ARCHITECTS' HOMES

ARCHITECTS' HOMES

Edited by Bethany Patch

images
Publishing

Published in Australia in 2017 by
The Images Publishing Group Pty Ltd
ABN 89 059 734 431
6 Bastow Place, Mulgrave, Victoria 3170, Australia
Tel: +61 3 9561 5544 Fax: +61 3 9561 4860
books@imagespublishing.com
www.imagespublishing.com

The Images Publishing Group Reference Number: 1157

National Library of Australia Cataloguing-in-Publication entry:

Title:	Architects' Homes / edited by Bethany Patch
ISBN:	9781864706086 (hardback)
Subjects:	Architects—Homes and haunts.
	Architecture, Domestic.
Dewey Number:	728.37

Production manager: Rod Gilbert
Senior editor: Gina Tsarouhas
Coordinating editor: Bethany Patch
Graphic designers: Nicole Boehringer and Ryan Marshall

Page 3: Model of Summer House in Dalarna, image courtesy of Leo Qvarsebo

Printed on 140gsm GoldEast Matt Art paper by Everbest Printing Co. Ltd., in Hong Kong/China

Contents

Introduction

The home is a built form that allows the architect to explore and convert ideas into reality. The opportunities and potential for expression to expand the boundaries of building form and building space are endless. We, as humans, occupy this space. One type of architecture that we have grown over time to accept—to the point that it is now essential to our wellbeing and survival—is shelter, a place we can call home, whether it is in an urban, human-made context, or more connected to nature.

Architects use the design of their own homes both as a design experiment and as a representation of their own beliefs and ideals. Their grounding through education and experience may form a base or starting point, but the influences of their culture, lifestyle and the environment of their upbringing are naturally integrated into their architecture. In places where the light is soft and gray, expanses of glass flood the rooms with natural light. In places where the sun is bright and harsh, either walls are dominant, or openings and expanses of glass are shaded with screens.

The scale of the single-family house is the primary building form that allows, and in many cases encourages, the architect to both develop and experiment with an idea or ideas that include or expand their own awareness of light, space, form and context. The architects' design positions are diverse, the context is diverse and cultures are varied. The customized house is a "one off," an architect's interpretation of design equated with the needs and values of the owner's family and their sense of a home. It is tailored to the architect's own family's program, balanced by the architect's personal design perspective. In the Steinhaus (Stone House; page 172), by Günther Domenig, the design is personal and "the house is at the same time my body—my feeling—my thinking." With the advent of the digital age, the future may be less defined. We can now be attached to our home without actually being there. Automation is, and will continue to be, changing the house in ways that we have not even thought of. The new norm is change.

The fit of an architect's house within a context is occasionally controversial, but the opposite is also true, where the context is improved by the addition of a house. The translucent skin of the exterior walls of the Slip House (page 158), by Carl Turner, which is built on what once was a brownfield site, consists of three stacked boxes stepped outwards thereby reducing the sense of the mass, but it visualizes lightness by melding the form with the sky behind. In the Welham Studios residence (page 202), by Mark Merer, the difficult task of locating the house in a meadow is achieved by carrying the meadow over the roof of the house so that when viewed from the meadow the house is invisible; it is an integral part of the meadow.

The size of an architect's own home is often an expression of their professional commitment. There is a small but current movement towards the micro unit, an expression of a need to achieve home ownership, however small. At the opposite scale, the MacMansion is still popular, but architects' homes tend to be more responsible and they generally scale the size of their home as a direct relationship to their needs. The exception may be the inclusion of a home studio, where they can work at home at the weekends and still be part of the family activities. On the other hand, the library of books or the two-story living room with a mezzanine have either been reduced in size or scale, or eliminated altogether in contrast with the increased integration of automation in the house.

The rooms in a single-family house are defined and your sense of the space reinforced by how the enclosure surfaces, the walls, floor and ceiling, form and wrap the room or space. A critical element in defining or expressing a room are the corners, the room is now contained, it has a boundary. A second critical element is the floor and ceiling. Is the floor level, is the ceiling raised. Once the space is defined by the enclosure surfaces, the room is still not visible to the human eye without light, either daylight or nightlight. How light is introduced into a room through openings in the exterior surfaces both defines the space and provides the room with its most prominent identity. The light that enters a room through the placement of openings, windows and skylights defines how a person experiences the room. By not placing the window on axis with the door, this will initially contain your vision when you enter a room. You will experience the room before your eyes wander and recognize the architectural details or the furniture and other objects placed in the room. Frank Lloyd Wright placed windows in the corners of a room specifically to eliminate the room's defining element, thereby both expanding the dimensions of a room and to include the landscape beyond. This strong connection between the inside and outside is seen in the corner window of Wooloowin House (page 209) in Queensland, by Terry McQuillan. The roof is a fifth elevation. It is the one surface that receives the most light. The size, shape and placement of a skylight can alter the mood of a room, as the light source is ever moving. Light from above has an uplifting feeling, similar to the light source in a Gothic cathedral. These are just the beginning and a small part of the architect's vocabulary and dictionary of elements that create a room or space.

With the minimalist movement, clarity in the design of the room or space is the dominant element. The addition of furniture may deconstruct the expression and power of the room as the objects in the space begin to cloud the focus of the room, a fireplace, paintings on the walls, the furniture or the grand piano. But occupying the room this way may personalize the space and provide that all-important sense of ownership for the owner. A home that now belongs to the family.

The vertical dimension is also an important element in the definition of a room. The two-story room lifts your eye upwards. This effect can also be achieved in a more modest manner by allowing light to enter the room through a skylight. The light source from a hidden skylight with inclined walls and reflected light descending into the room introduces a sense of mystery and emotion to the room. Ricardo Legorreta always talks of how his houses are designed to evoke a feeling of emotion from the occupant.

As you move from one room to another your eyes are contained by the design of the room. You are not aware of the next room before you have experienced the room that you have just entered. Now the element of circulation has been introduced, the act of a person moving from one room to another or through space. The primary controlling element in circulation is where and how you enter the room, the placement of the door or entry. By placing the entrance threshold at a corner, the diagonal view makes the room appear larger than it really is. By placing the door in the center, you achieve symmetry or balance. Even in an open plan the point of entry is critical. What do you first observe from this entry.

The boundaries of interior space are expanded and exterior space captured through the transparency of the exterior wall. With walls of glass, the exterior space is integrated with and extends the sense of the room. In the Brick Country house designed by Ludwig Mies van der Rohe in 1923, the wall extends out into the landscape, thereby blurring the definition of where the interior ends and the exterior begins. In the Farnsworth house by Mies, the glass walls that wrap the house further blurs the definition of the exterior, as the exterior wall becomes the landscape itself. The Tower House (page 183), by Thomas Gluck, achieves this relationship with an exterior wall of glass, which during the day reflects the surrounding woods, camouflaging the house, but at night, the transparency of the glass de-materializes the form. Alternatively, instead of expanding out into the landscape, the house can partially or wholly contain an exterior space by surrounding the space and forming a courtyard or atrium. The Courtyard is a traditional house form in several countries and can expand the house by forming an additional functional room. The Architects' House + Studio (page 18) in New Delhi, by Manit Rastogi and Sonali Rastogi, successfully incorporates the courtyard as if it were an additional room in the house.

The architect's palette and selection of materials is nearly endless, with the more traditional materials of concrete, stone, metal, wood, and glass, and the more flexible materials of plywood, plastic and plaster are now supplemented with a fairly endless list of new and composite materials. Infinitesimal designs and forms are now possible with this array of materials. But materials need space to breathe and to be appreciated. Occasionally a primary material can be contrasted or highlighted with a second material. The concrete structure in the Skyline Drive 1 residence (page 152), by Feras Gabriel Raffoul, is contrasted with the smooth plaster walls with a sheen finish. This traditional surface material is usually smooth or has an even texture, but now architects are also exploring ways of modulating this surface, even with traditional tools.

The moral responsibility today and in the future is to tread more lightly on the land and to reduce our personal consumption. With this objective in mind, we are also becoming more optimistic. The move towards the zero energy house—with more effective glazing, increased insulation and a reduction in electrical energy and water consumption— is not solely technical but illustrates how architects respond in their selection and use of low energy consumption materials. Architects are at the forefront of the sustainable and energy reduction movement. How is the house oriented towards the sun to take advantage of the sun's heat when needed, but also protected from the sun with shading when the sun's heat is not needed? For a precedent see the Villa Girasole in northern Italy. The house, built between 1929 and 1935, and is designed in the shape of a "V," is lifted up and placed on a turntable with large wheels, which allows the whole house to rotate on a spindle that contains the circular staircase. The courtyard contained within the "V" plan faces and tracks the sun, thereby taking advantage of the sun's warming rays in winter. In Ash+Ash (page 30), by Timothy Eddy, high-performance sustainable design features include a geo-exchange heat pump that circulates water in underground pipes to utilize the constant year-round ground temperature to warm or cool the house.

The architectural design elements that expand one's awareness of interior and exterior spaces and the iconic image of "home" are so diverse and numerous that the single-family house has become the archetype for the positive exploration of new spatial ideas and forms that reflect the various cultures and personal traits of the owners. The houses that follow represent a small segment of the designs that result from a successful collaboration between the architect as the designer and the architect as the owner.

John V Mutlow, FAIA
Professor
ACSA Distinguished Professor
Director, Global Studies, University of Southern California

Projects

ZH·1173

The architects, **Andreas Fuhrimann** and **Gabrielle Hächler**, of Andreas Fuhrimann Gabrielle Hächler Architekten, wanted to build four reasonably priced apartments for themselves and their friends and family. Their **Apartment at the Foot of the Üetliberg mountain**, in Zurich, Switzerland, was designed with high standards of living comfort, ensuring that each of the four apartments benefited as much as possible whether facing the impressive views to the north or south. The structure of the design and choice of materials resulted in a striking appearance. The two double-story apartments and the two roof apartments are encapsulated in each other so that each angle of the four-sided building is fully utilized.

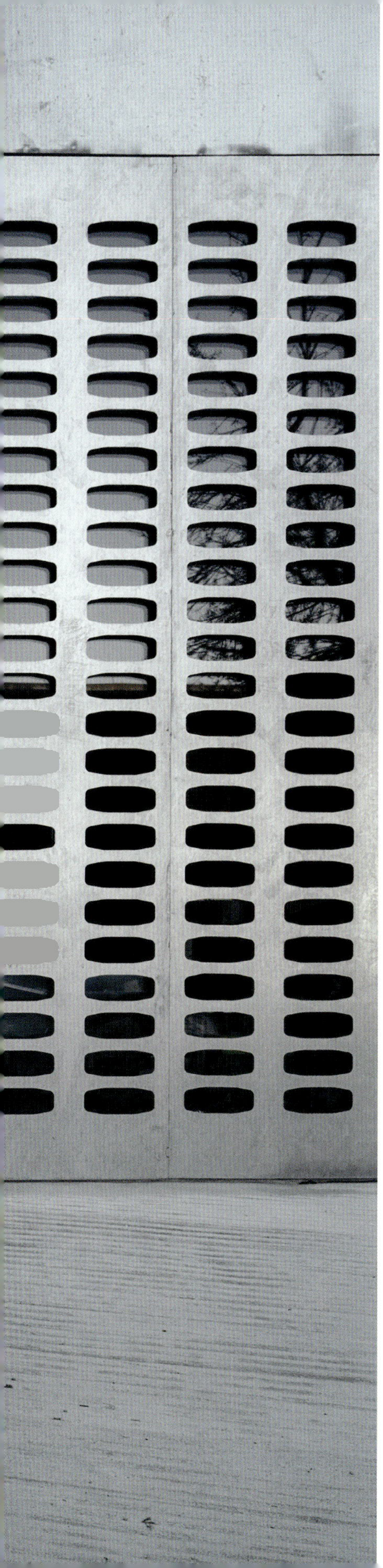

The architects wanted to create a low-budget building that deliberately emphasized the use of materials. Commonplace and unrefined materials such as concrete, timber, wood and galvanized steel were used, which animate one another when combined. For example, the intentional combination of color and reflective glass surfacing in the kitchens, and extensive glass paneling of the walls in the bathrooms, contrast with coarse concrete and organic wood patterning. The basement, stairwells and partitioning walls, which are made of concrete cast, counterbalance the acoustic radiance of the timber elements. This concrete core acts as the skeleton of the wooden structure, with the organic softness of the wood heightening the rawness of the concrete.

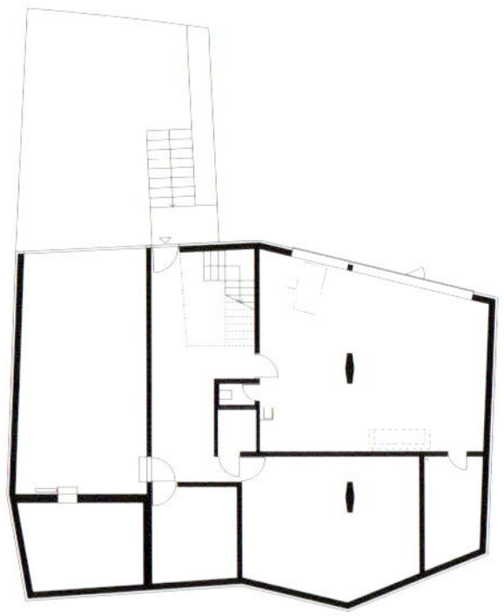

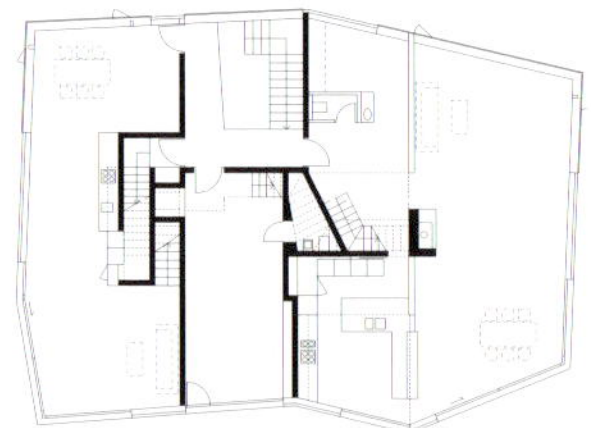

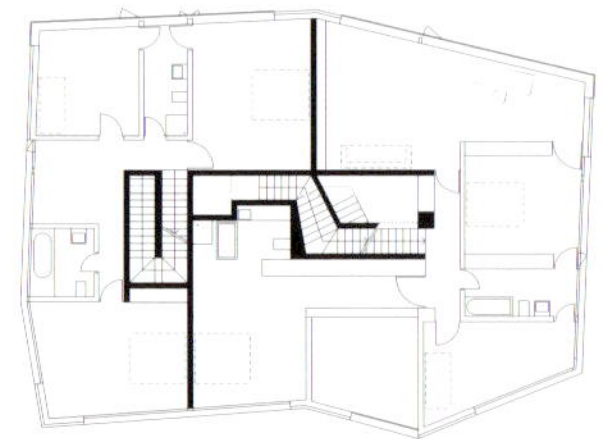

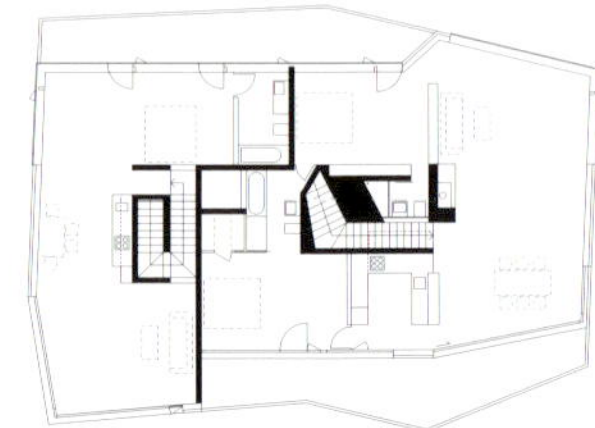

The architects utilized the current technologies of prefabrication—with complex spatial structures and polygonal geometry—to achieve a rapid assembly of only three days. The most striking element of the galvanized sheet-metal façade is the differentiation of the form of the window openings on the north and south sides. The polygonal and sharp-edged volume of the building is accentuated by its external skin of large-format, galvanized-metal panels. This building has a crystalline and compact expression.

Photography: *Valentin Jeck*

Architects' House + Studio, in New Delhi, India, is unique because it manages the convergence of two specific ideals within Indian house design and architecture: the modern family as a social unit (with associated comforts) and the environment. Here, the architects **Manit Rastogi** and **Sonali Rastogi**, of Morphogenesis, illustrate that the challenges of shifting traditions, and necessity to address local and global environmental changes, can be met with architectural creativity.

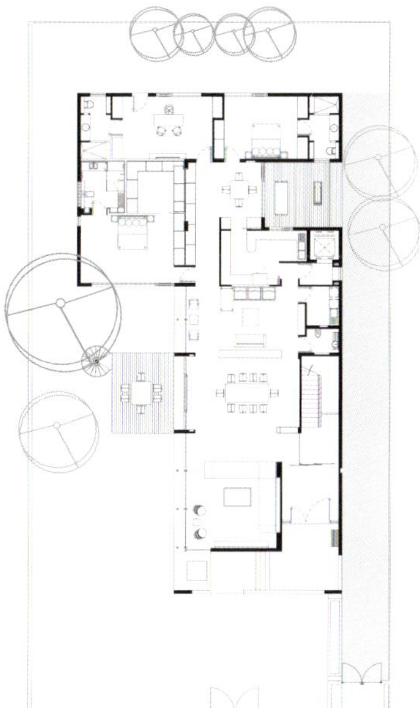

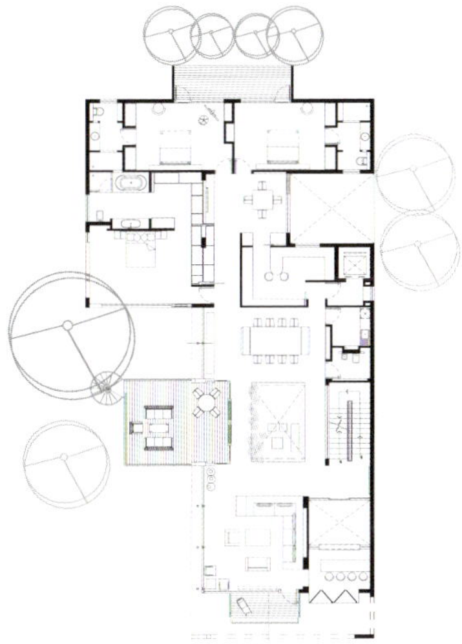

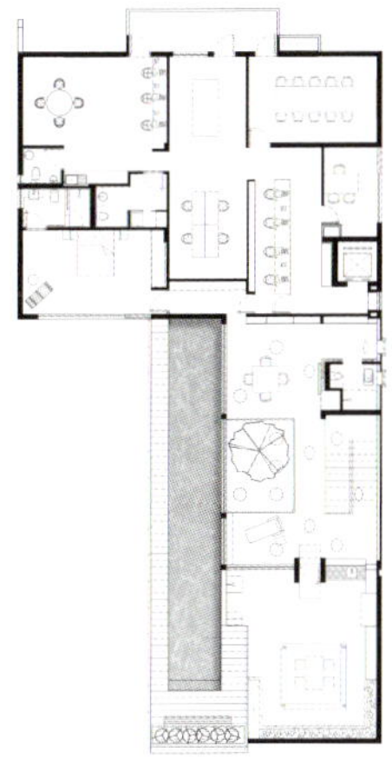

This mixed-use home shelters three generations of their family and the studio of the architects, while also functioning as a social space for visitors. The architects' parents are among those who live at the house, whose abode is situated close to the impressive landscaped gardens. The outdoor green spaces are brought into the house with an interior garden, allowing fresh air and natural light into the internal volumes.

The spatial layout of the house is split into three distinct categories: private family space, shared inter-generational areas and the public domains. The central space acts as the pivoting, social and energetic core of the house. The materials used in construction are renewable resources: timbers, rice paper, glass, and so on. Water acts as a material resource, allowing for the reflection and dispersion of natural light.

The environmental design of the house, in response to its suitability in the Delhi climate, was an integral component for the architects. The house can be imagined as a permeable fixture, with fresh air and visual connectivity breathing through the indoor and outdoor spaces. Elements of the design that work together to improve the environmental footprint of the space include glazed glass to the north, high thermal mass to the west (which aids thermal regulation in all seasons), landscape buffers to the south and high performance surfaces to the east. The architects have created a responsive ecosystem that reflects the specific needs of an extensive family.

Photography: *Amit Mehra and Edmund Sumner*

When designing their own home, architects can exercise the courage and satisfaction of curating a space specifically for themselves and their family's needs. **Argyle**, designed and built by **David Saunders** (of architectural firm S2 design) is exemplary of this. Situated in St Kilda, Melbourne, Saunders chose to revitalize this heritage home for his young family, adding a new rear section that incorporates several salvaged elements of the original Victorian structure. Saunders's aim was to leave the finished materials appearing as unchanged as possible from the vitality of the original—less white paint, more timber paneling, and natural materials. Saunders was also the builder for the project, which enabled a more hands-on approach without the heavy use of architectural drawings.

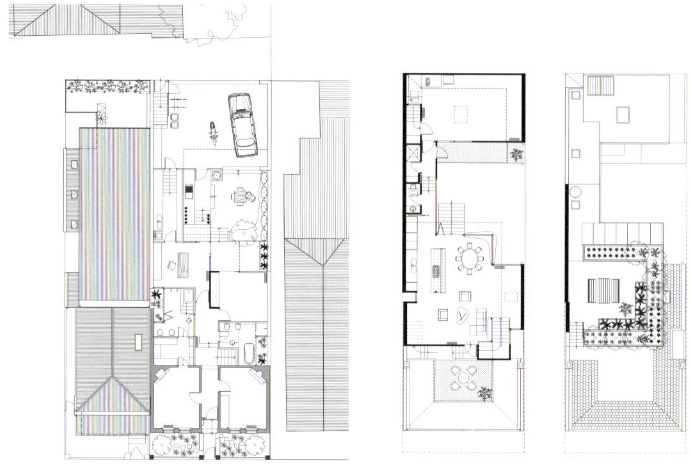

The design of the house evolved throughout the build, often in response to changing site conditions or the addition of the architect's own art collection. The site is approximately 28.5 feet (8.7 meters) wide, with a rear lane for vehicle access, and a level difference of 5 feet (1.5 meters) between the street and the higher rear lane. The front two rooms of the existing Victorian house were kept to maintain the existing heritage streetscape. The new, rear structure comprises ten changes in level, and a number of those levels are wrapped around a central courtyard, which allows the early morning sun to brighten the house throughout winter. The roof level was designed to support 200 tons of soil, where Saunders has provided his family with a productive "roof farm."

The design is environmentally sophisticated, collecting over 11,360 gallons (43,000 liters) of rainwater in four tanks in the basement, under the garage. These tanks supply water to the entire dwelling, and are also connected to evacuated tubes that provide 70 percent of the hot water for the house. The design is also very personal, with Saunders's collection of artworks having been worked into the structure, as well as bathroom gardens as part of the natural ventilation system. David Saunders brings panache and integrity to this complex and innovative home, which reflects his personal creativity in architecture and construction.

This text was originally written by Don Gazzard and has been edited by Bethany Patch.

Photography: *John Gollings*

At **Ash+Ash**, owner and architect **Timothy Eddy**, of Hennebery Eddy Architects, wanted to inspire others through uncompromised contemporary architecture that was seamlessly integrated with high-performance sustainable design. The house is sited on Mount Tabor, the only extinct volcano within a United States city—in Portland, Oregon.

The design sustains a close relationship with its immediate environment, taking advantage of sweeping views of Portland and surrounding mountains. In response to diverse weather patterns, the parti stems from a desire to create a range of terraces and porches for use at different times of the day. Central to the design concept is the desire to blur the lines between the outdoor spaces and the interior through extensive transparency.

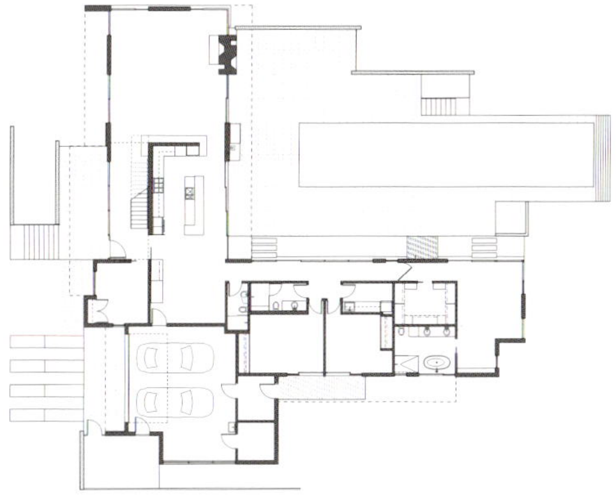

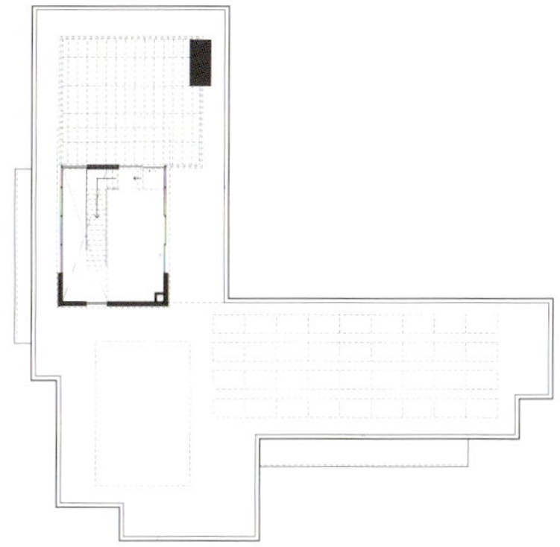

6620

The L-shaped plan places main living and gathering spaces in a separate wing from guest and master bedroom spaces and encloses a visually private pool terrace. The core of the living wing is wrapped in rift-cut white oak and complemented by a cantilevered walnut stair to a rooftop viewbox. Interior walls and lighting are proportioned to display Eddy's collected artwork. Ash+Ash features expansive glass walls, an open plan, and strong horizontal lines. The result is a home that draws heavily on the tenets of Modernism. Deep cedar soffits protect glazing from the sun and extend to the interior forming a more intimate enclosure in the guest bedrooms, master bath, and rooftop viewbox.

In addition to impressive construction nuances, this project incorporates a geo-exchange heat pump, under-floor radiant heating, triple glazing, LED lighting, exterior blinds to control heat gain, rainwater recovery, solar panels and solar pool heating. Certified as LEED (Leadership in Energy and Environmental Design) Platinum, this home is one of open space and sophisticated design elements.

Photography: Josh Partee

Australian architects **Mark** and **Angela Jamison**, of Jamison Architects, designed **Bird House**, completed in 2015, as a home for their young family. Situated on the Gold Coast of Queensland, Australia, this unique design is surrounded by bushland and tall gum trees. Architecturally, the intention here was to maintain a strong connection to the site and its natural environment, including an abundance of native flora and fauna.

From the sloping, elevated landscape on which the home is built, the upper living spaces have the feeling of being in a birdhouse among the trees, with open and light interior spaces that allow the natural light and sounds of the bush into the internal environment of the house. In this way, the design brings the outdoors in, maximizing the views to the trees, skyline and hinterland, maintaining their privacy, and utilizing the benefits of natural light and cross-ventilation with a passive solar design. Essentially, the structure comprises two pavilions connected by a central grassed courtyard. The courtyard changes dimensions throughout the day and night; by day, it offers shade and filtered light through the screens; by night, it frames the sky and provides a stunning outdoor room to spend time together as a family—in front of a fire, watching films or star-gazing. Enclosed by operable screens, the space can be made intimate and closed or open and connected to the surrounding landscape.

The floor plan is highly efficient and retains a feeling of spaciousness with the use of a void and floor-to-ceiling glazing. There is a beautiful flow between the indoor and outdoor spaces, and Jamison has incorporated elements that are both interesting and practical to the design. Angela and Mark have designed an enjoyable space where they can spend quality time with their family and the environment.

Photography: *Scott Burrows Photographer*

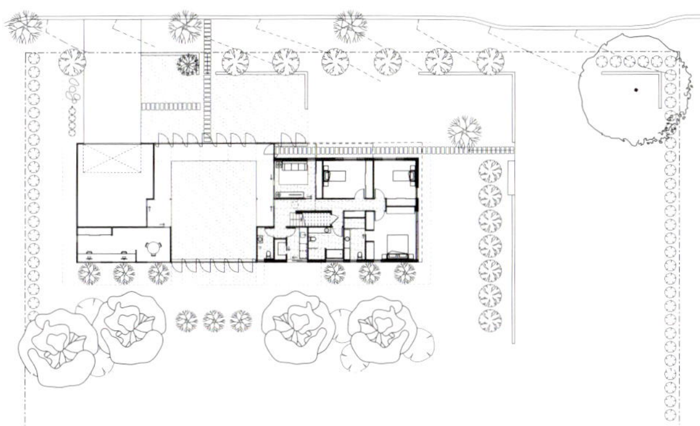

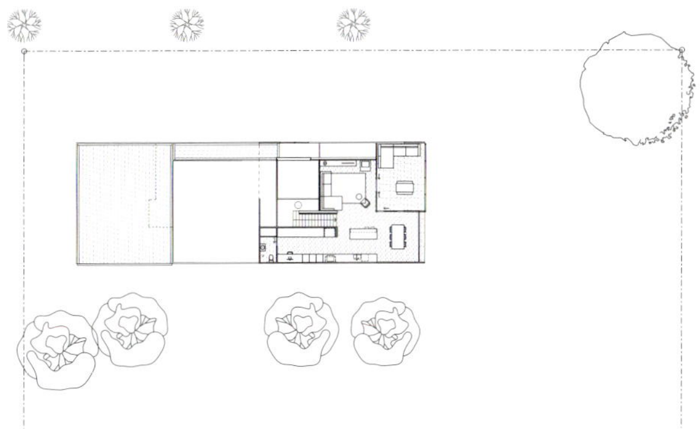

As a family, we feel connected to our environment and to each other within the home.

Angela and Mark Jamison

The design of this project, **Casa CM** by architect **Paolo Carlesso**, provided the architect with an opportunity to design and construct his own home in an innovative and anti-cyclical way, in an attempt to radicalize techniques of architectural design. The desire and necessity to construct with methods that utilize sustainable materials and construction practices, and that are also economic and require minimal labor, dictated all of the architect's design decisions.

My trees are still twigs, my sons are still children, my house is not finished yet, there is still a little something to be done, everyday life is magic.

Paolo Carlesso

The house is a very simple design—measuring a modest 3120 square feet (290 square meters). Sophisticated and interesting elements are positioned with precision throughout, including strong visual lines (both internally and externally) and blocks of juxtaposing raw materials. With gray external boards, and an interior of rendered concrete and wooden paneling, the architect's design is both thoughtful and considered, and integrates beautifully with the site.

The skeleton of the house is a steel frame, and the exterior comprises a ventilated façade made from eco-fiber cement. The walls of the house consist of interlocking timber panels, assembled without the use of any adhesives. The architect's desire was to embrace and enhance the history of this site, refusing the contemporary urban expansion model of many other houses in the area. Here, in the town of Fagnano Olona, Italy, orientation and location are dictated by rural architecture, with building typology and finishing materials inspired by industrial expansion.

The organization of the site, the economy of the materials selected, and the self-construction of the building are all factors congruent with the period of re-colonization of the land that occurred at the hands of the immigrants in the mid 1990s. There were also substantial financial benefits of the personal build, which was funded by the architect himself.

Photography: *Simone Bossi*

The natural contrasts on this site provide the inspiration for the architecture of **C-House**, by **Robert Maschke**, FAIA, of Robert Maschke Architects. This house is a striking, unique home in the Detroit Shoreway neighborhood in Cleveland's near west side, Ohio. Despite the industrial setting of this community, this particular site is a tranquil enclave within park-like land on its southern and eastern borders. With a beautiful tree-lined boulevard close by, and views of Lake Erie and downtown Cleveland, this design reconnects the site to its local environment.

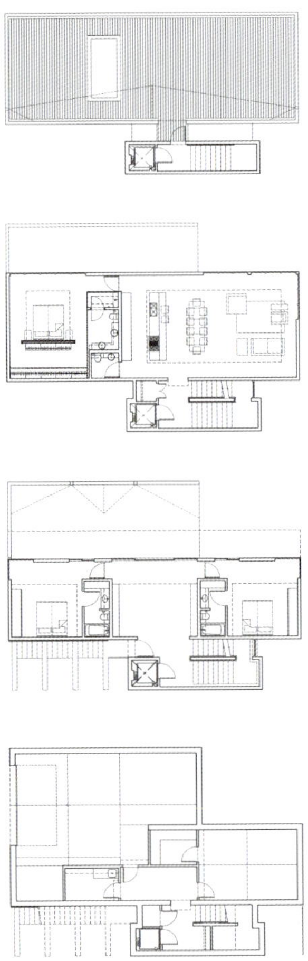

This design utilizes a stacked program, providing each of the interior living areas with the best view possible. This sectional strategy results in a cantilever, which ensures that the exterior spaces below are sheltered, while also creating an intriguing element of architecture. In order to resourcefully frame each of the views, fenestration is employed. The result is an expression that contrasts in opacity with each new elevation, with a differing character to its setting—nestled into the hill with its bold, white form. This unique structure has an iconic presence for anyone who has the privilege of passing by.

Photography: *Hanson Photographic*

Ben Edwards, of Edwards Moore, extended a modest workers cottage in Fitzroy, Melbourne, into the **Doll's House**. Measuring only 13 by 75.5 feet (4 by 23 meters), the Doll's House appears surprisingly spacious—choreographed gold panels throughout the space echo the history of the home and provide the illusion that there is more space on the other side of each wall. Edwards has preserved the initial street frontage and primary living areas, whilst fragmenting the extension beyond with the inclusion of two courtyards that both separate and connect the modern functions for living.

There are no doors to obstruct one's walk from one end of the extension to the other, resulting in a long passageway along the southern side of the house. This ensures that visual and spatial connections are maintained through all living spaces.

On the northern side of the house, the two courtyard gardens are essential to creating the illusion of increased space, while also flooding the interior rooms with sunlight and natural ventilation, and acting as circulation zones that open the house to the garden. Glass doors to the exterior ensure constant views between the courtyards and interior rooms, which, along with an open plan between the rooms, assist in increasing the perceived size inside the home.

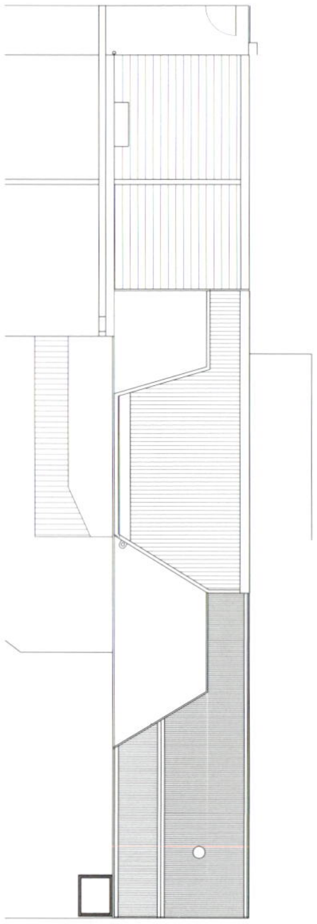

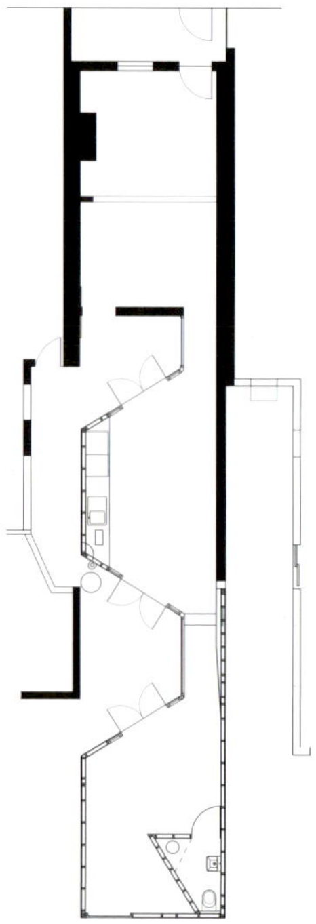

A symphony of raw and untreated finishes creates an aesthetic that complements Edwards's desire for a simple living style. There is an abundance of sunlight that enters through the courtyard and refracts off all the white interior surfaces, creating a sense of playfulness that is hidden from the busy urban setting outside. The seemingly unassuming Doll's House harbors sophisticated detail in its design and composition of materials forming a functional, rustic, yet industrial atmosphere.

Photography: Fraser Marsden

I like this house as it's a work in progress, which allows things to evolve and change.

Ben Edwards

Jetty and Maarten Min, partner architects of Dutch architecture and design firm Min2, designed **Dune House**, a highly unique and sustainable home with a striking appearance. Dune House aims to connect form and materialization with the natural environment in which it is situated. The three-story house enjoys a dominant position on a dune crest in Bergen, the Netherlands, where its tall, rounded form blends well with the neighboring dune and tall pine trees that guard it.

The house, with a gross floor area of 3770 square feet (350 square meters), sits only 985 feet (300 meters) from the sea. Therefore, the architects believed it required "low-tech" materials—ones that are natural, sustainable and low-maintenance. For the oblique façade and roof skin, they wanted a material that would create a balance with the romance of the scenery.

Jetty herself designed a long, flat clay tile that matched these criteria, based on the Kolumba bricks designed by Swiss architect Peter Zumthor. The brown coloring of the British clay perfectly aligns with its surrounding environment. The eaves are finished with zinc to match the clay tiles, and the untreated wooden frames are handpicked for the longest sections to avoid as much adhesive as possible.

The openings in the roof surface were designed especially to appreciate the view that they each face—to the sea as horizontal strips and to the dune as one huge window, where one can immerse oneself in the landscape. The upper rooms of the house have the advantage of marvelous views of the dunes and sea. Throughout the construction, Jetty and Maarten were careful to impact on the surrounding environment as little as possible. The design of the house and the interior spaces were decided with meticulous care and attention to sustainable detail. The result is a home that reflects the architects' personalities, and acts as a laboratory for new developments and concepts in home design and architecture.

Photography: Bodo Mertoglu (interior) and Erik Boschman (exterior)

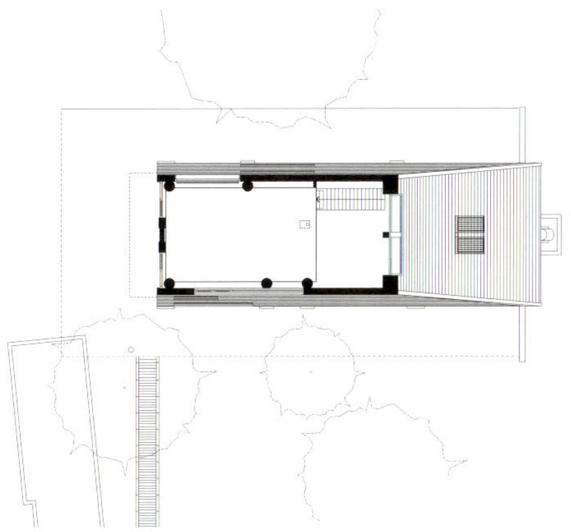

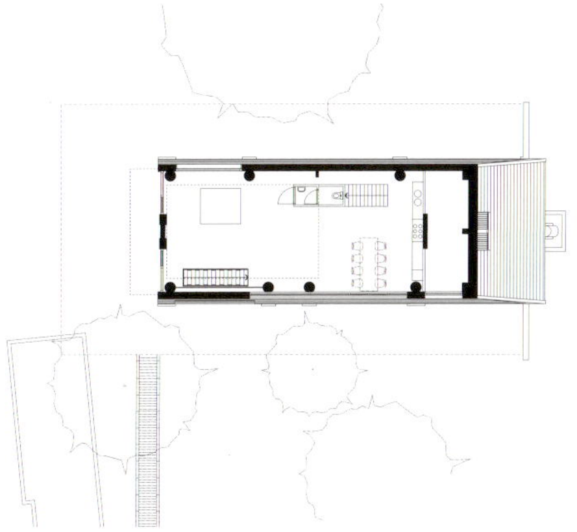

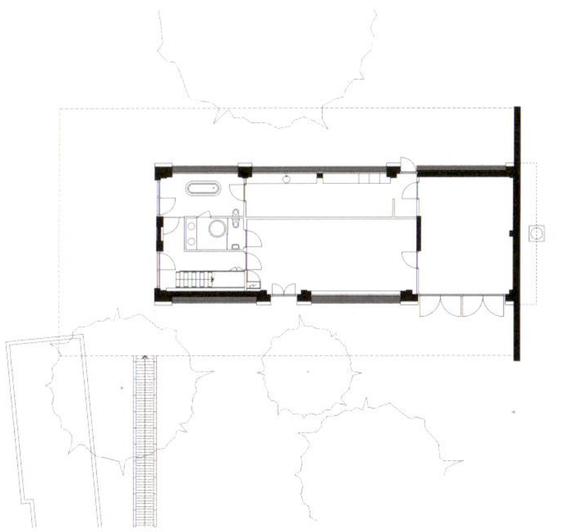

The simple and sophisticated design of the **Garden Street Residence** in East Austin, Texas, harmonizes a pure Modernist style with the traditional barn and stable structures found throughout the United States, particularly in the rural south. Designed and owned by **Shane Pavonetti** of Pavonetti Architecture, this small home is a symbiotic collection of wrought aesthetic and rustic interiors—cedar siding, exposed wooden and steel framing and steel windows, with the Modernist touch of spacious interiors, large windows, clean lineation, and trim-less detail.

A respect for the environment, as well as a celebration of the unpolished industrial textures of construction, is built into the very fabric of the house. The house boasts a handmade staircase, which was constructed onsite from recycled long leaf pine, expanded metal, and plate steel.

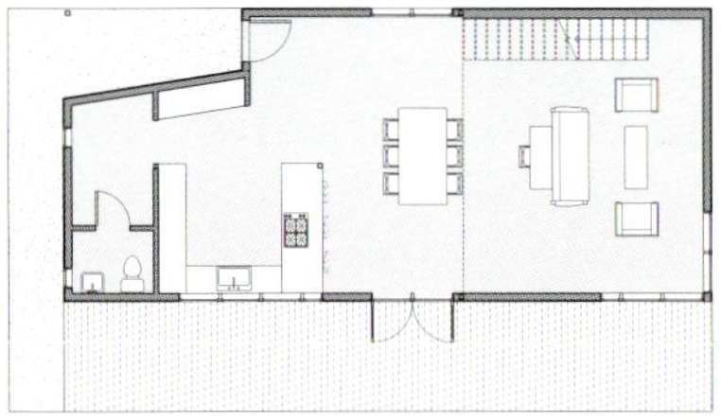

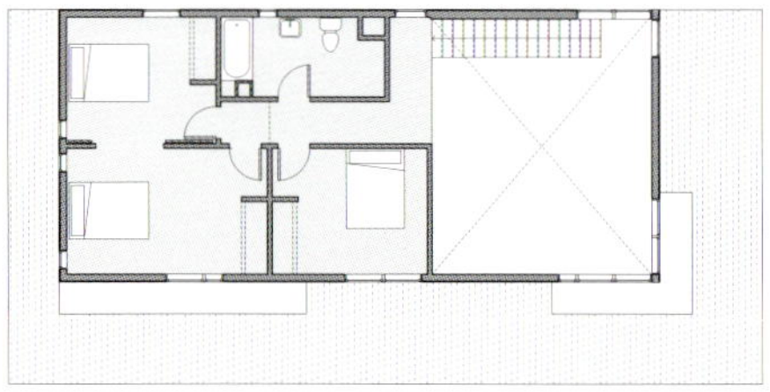

The long windows were constructed only 2 miles (3.2 kilometers) from the site, reducing the carbon footprint of the property during construction. Any remaining steel from the construction was reformed into interior fittings for the house, for example, pedestal sink tables and entry tables. The foundation of the house, a concrete slab, was left untouched on the lower floor, with tongue-and-groove framing lumber that was used as the decking and final floor surface for the upper level.

The designs of the interiors were focused on showcasing the space with a simple elegance, in the same way that the home was designed. The interior colors are often juxtaposing dark features against light walls and floor, with additional elements kept as minimal as possible. Soft lighting (with styled light fittings), raw wooden benches, bold colored furniture and intentional placement of indoor plants soften the space and contextualize the house based on Pavonetti's personality.

***Photography:** Amanda Kirkpatrick*

Glass House, designed by **Thomas Roszak** for his family of three children, has a simple objective: to push the boundaries of everyday living forward into the future. Roszak's intentions were to build this 8820-square-foot (820-square-meter) home on a modest budget while providing a forward-thinking aesthetic with the space. This house experiments with transparency and reflectivity, while showcasing open, undivided spaces that are filled with natural light.

The home also needed to be built as an efficient smart house in its construction, energy use and lifestyle, for both Roszak as architect and builder and for Roszak's family. With each variable of user control to be reduced to the touch of a digital button (lights, shades, communication/audio, security and air control), and the inclusion of a high performance curtain-wall, the house has developed as a low-impact environment with advanced technological functions. A planning module was developed that is based on a square room that measures 16 feet (4.9 meters) on each side. This "interstitial space" is utilized for hallways, bathrooms and stairways, and ensures that the active rooms remain pure and uncluttered.

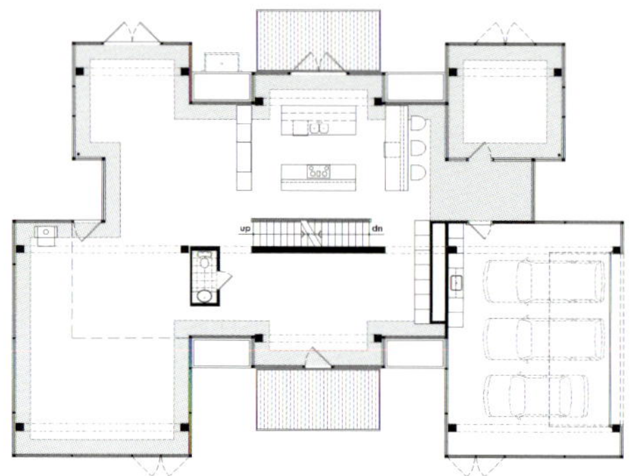

The interior furnishing style incorporates custom-built pieces with classic and new items that have been collected, and in some cases designed personally, by Roszak. The trinity of sharp coloring—in the bright red lacquer, Brazilian cherry floorboards and yellow steel—enables a warmth to exude from the interior spaces, especially when contrasting them with the precision of the architecture.

The house openly amalgamates the interior spaces with the exterior environment. The result is a very remarkable façade, where the mathematical calculation of the house design extends through into the layout of the wooded grounds—the single acre (half hectare) of vegetation and hardscapes. Roszak has succeeded in bringing elements of comfort and warmth to a unique, transparent space. This home received the American Institute of Architect's Honor Award for interior architecture in 2008.

Photography: Hedrich Blessing Photography

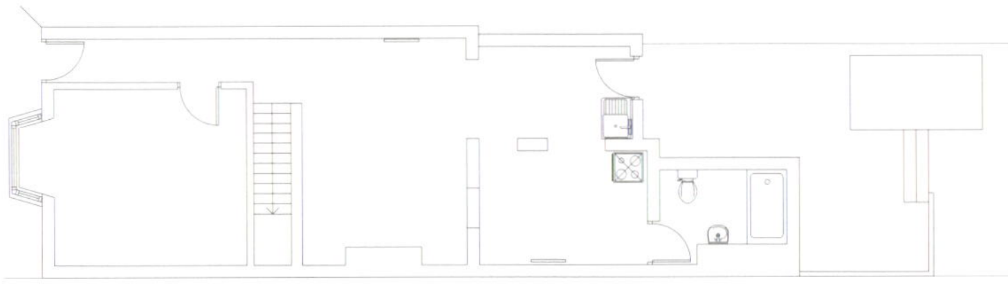

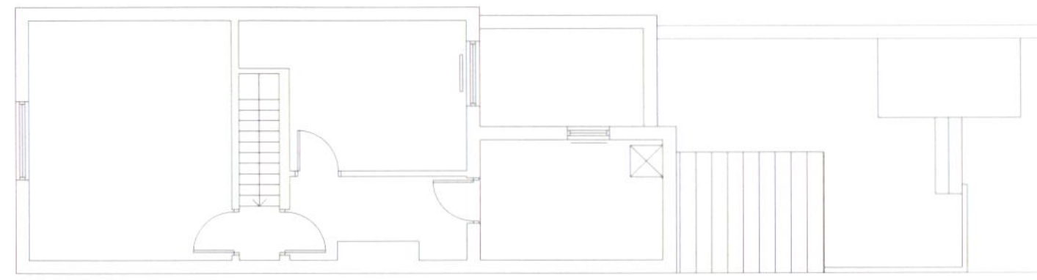

Greenbank Road, designed by **Federica Vasetti** for herself and her partner, Jens Marklof, is a remarkable and creative extension project in Bristol, England. The existing, terraced Victorian house was originally constructed in 1875 to house the influx of tobacco factory workers at the time. Vasetti's goals for the new house were simple: space for a family, a studio in the home, generous open plan living, and lots of natural light. Several previous owners had altered the property in an ad hoc fashion that resulted in a sequence of dark rooms disconnected from the garden. The desire to achieve open internal spaces within a limited English terrace house was integral to the design of the new home.

The extended elements include a ground floor extension of 290 square feet (27 square meters), relocated kitchen, internal insulation, and new bathroom, flooring, plumbing, wiring and landscaping. The new design incorporates a long hallway from the front door that leads to a large open plan kitchen–dining–living area. This open space was achieved by relocating the kitchen completely and extending the space into the former yard. To highlight the exterior space, the new roof rises toward the yard, opening up views and producing the appearance of an independent pavilion rather than an appendix to the house. Reclaimed timber rafters and beams support the roof and are left exposed to provide a focal element to the new living room. To reduce the impact on the neighboring properties, the corner of the new façade is chamfered, creating a striking contemporary statement. The timber cladding extends to the garden wall to define a covered decked area, which marks the transition between the interior and the beautiful landscaped garden.

Photography: *Federica Vasetti*

In Greek, hemeroscopium represents the place of the setting sun. An imaginary illusion, it is understood to us only in the context of the horizon, and our expectations of it are defined by its physical limitations, as well as light and time. **Hemeroscopium House**, designed and owned by architect **Antón García-Abril** of Ensamble Studio, is a playful representation of the ways in which our expectations of structure and form can be interrupted.

With heavy constructions and gravity-provoking shape placement, this house very much defines the site on which it sits. The structure is supported by a mother beam, with the ordered stack of shapes creating a helix that protrudes from it. The house comprises a total of seven elements, each relating to each of the others through a system of gravity and juxtaposition. The highly curated sequence becomes lighter as the structure proceeds upwards, culminating at a point of equilibrium with the other shapes. The result is a very unique and striking appearance that leaves the observer wondering how it retains its balance.

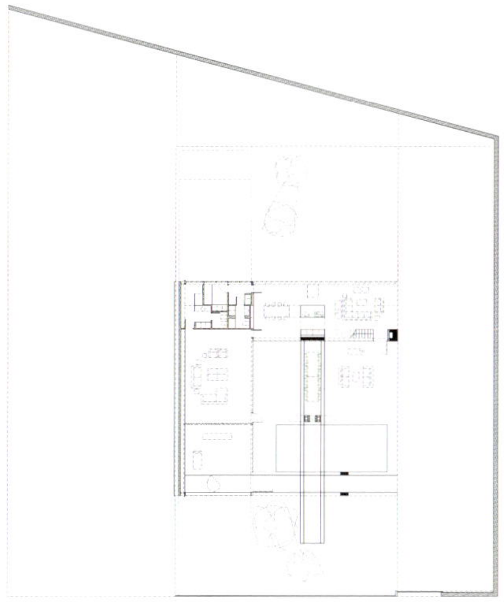

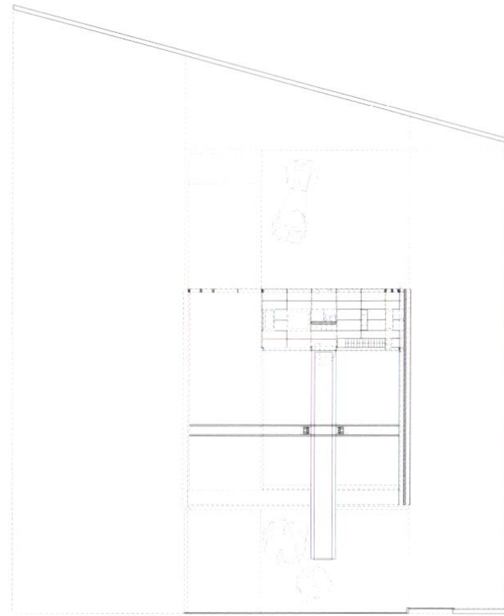

The joints were designed to respond to the forces of constructive nature and the stresses that are illustrated by their own structural positioning. While these joints express simplicity of form, they actually required numerous complicated and precise calculations regarding reinforcements and the pre- and post-tension of the steel beams. The way in which these elements are calculated and positioned culminates in a light, transparent and aerial structure. While the engineering of the house took a year, the structure was built in a remarkable seven days, due to a heavy reliance on prefabricated materials and an impeccably synchronized rhythm of assembly.

Photography: *Ensamble Studio and Roland Halbe*

On a rectangular 32,530-square-foot (3022-square-meter) plot in Ahmedabad, India, the **Ismet–Bimal Residence** sits parallel to the eastern edge, leaving a huge open space for a garden in the west-facing front yard. Designed for their extended family by architects **Ismet Khambatta** and **Bimal Patel** (of HCP Design Planning & Management), it is a long, linear house with a deep veranda that faces the garden, opening the interior spaces. Patel explains the significance of an architect's home, and its relation to the profession of architecture and design: "We envisaged a house that was simple, unassuming, comfortable and unostentatious."

The architects and their family (with two children and Khambatta's mother) live in this home and Patel is satisfied that the house has been seamlessly and effortlessly re-arranged around its occupants as they grow and change. The importance of family connection is represented all throughout the home, including the dining table of Khambatta's great grandfather. These multi-family homes are a common and significant element of Indian culture. The house opens each of its interior spaces toward the garden through a strong linear plan that incorporates the veranda, allowing constantly changing light to flood the house. There are no windows in the house, only large glazed doors and louvered panels that regulate light and air flow.

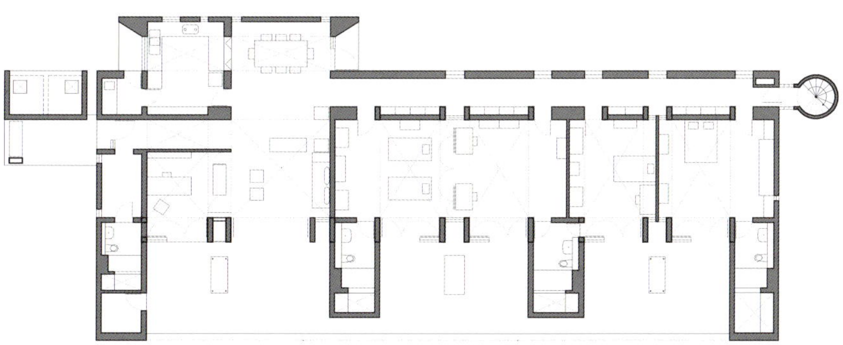

Patel confesses that there were cheerful disagreements between himself and Khambatta when designing the house, as to whether it should be designed as "architecture" or as a "home." However, the family-oriented orchestration of spaces, the open and spacious plan, and the connection to its surrounding environment, illustrate that the architects have guaranteed a perfect symbiosis of both. Patel claims that his favorite space in the house is the veranda: "Undoubtedly the veranda is the most magical part of the house. It connects the house with the garden. We live most of our lives here."

Photography: *Sachin Desai*

The house of an architect reflects their perception of a good life.

Bimal Patel

Among the impressive Dolomites mountain range of northeastern Italy, approximately 3350 feet (1020 meters) above sea level, sits Pliscia—a unique, agricultural hamlet with rich architectural traditions that have evolved over centuries. This hamlet represents a deep sense of community, where strong bonds of neighborhood assistance and solidarity remain essential characteristics today. It is within one of these unique communities that **Chalet La Pedevilla** is sited, designed and owned by architects **Armin Pedevilla** and **Caroline Willeit** for themselves and their three children.

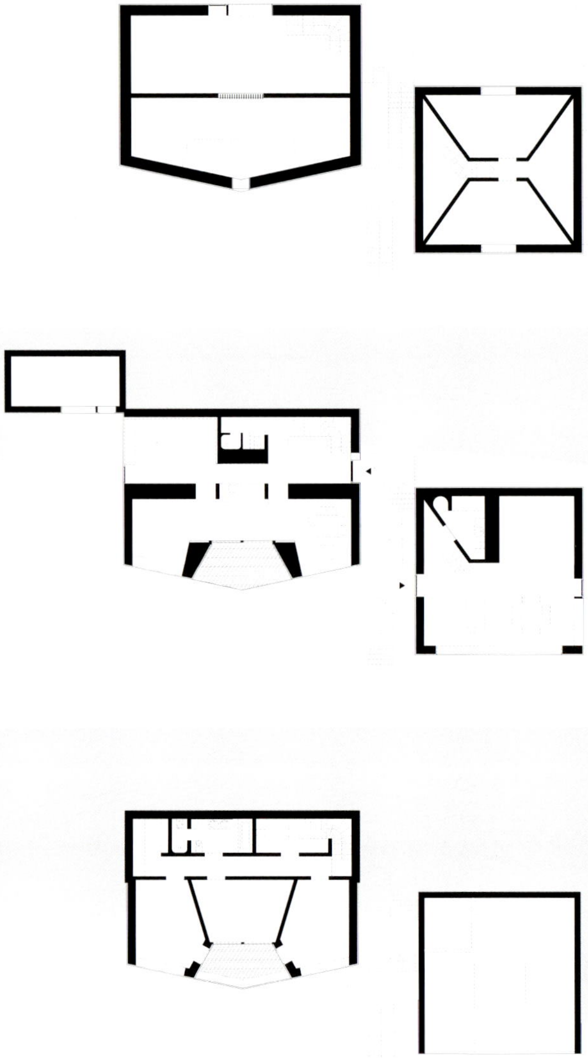

Usually, the old farmsteads of these hamlets would include a farmhouse with a subsidiary tenement. This project adheres to these deep-rooted traditions. Both buildings are integrated respectfully into the steep hillside. Locally specific design elements, such as the gabled roof, loggias and timber façade, were integrated into the design of this project but have been expressed in a singular and independent way. The architects specifically focused on the use of local materials in all structural elements of both buildings. Dolomite stone, the most common stone in this alpine region, was utilized as an aggregate with exposed concrete for the structural casts. Larch and pine timbers were cut from a nearby forest. The external timber frame with inbound loggias has been maintained. Contrasting black and white between exposed-concrete interior walls and ceilings, and natural and hand-hewn timber floors, windows, doors and furnitures make for a harmonious and striking interaction.

Sustainability and self-sufficiency remain the constants of life in the Dolomites hamlets, where these remote mountain regions rely on their own private water source and structures that provide independent energy (often through geothermal or solar power). This project is carefully considerate of traditional and cultural values, and is a reflection on the changing nature of ancient farming methods.

Photography: *Gustav Willeit*

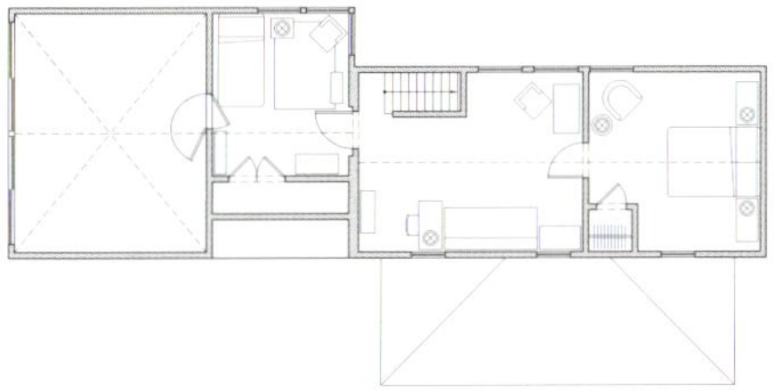

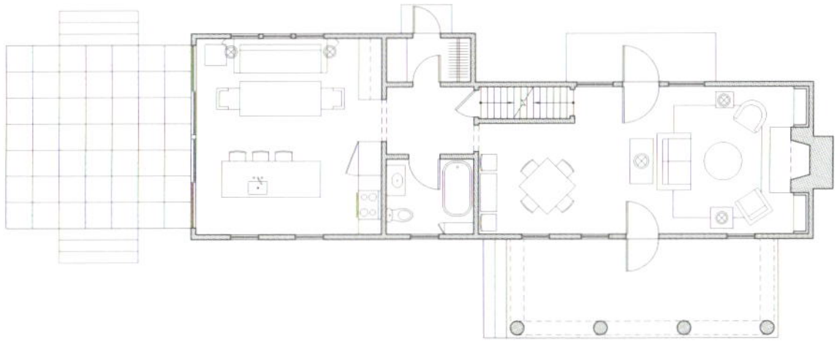

Douglas Larson designed the **Larson Residence** for himself and his wife and young son. Larson became interested in a dilapidated old farmhouse sited on a stunning backdrop of Stanfordville countryside in New York, United States. He began the design of this beautiful country retreat—a complete transformation of the existing structure, which was originally built in the late 18th or early 19th century. However, as almost no features of the original house remained (having been renovated several times before), this design was not constrained to the usual limitations of a historical renovation, freeing Larson to design more personally. Elements harvested for re-use were the two-over-two windows, some clapboard siding, an antique bathtub, and old board doors.

The existing, smaller interior rooms were replaced with larger spaces, and the structural beams and posts were exposed as an intentional design element. Of the previous wings of the house, the attic was transformed into a family kitchen and common space, and the gable end wall was glazed all the way to the ridge in order to provide as much natural light as possible. The former front porch, missing when Larson purchased the property, was reinstated using Doric columns. The roof was also replaced with metal panels, similar to the metal roofs of nearby agricultural buildings. The existing materials were reclaimed wherever possible, and highly effective insulation techniques were used when replacing any walls and glass, to ensure that the environmental impact of the building was kept to a minimum.

The effect is a gentle, handsome aesthetic that highlights the existing and new histories of the house, and is juxtaposed beautifully against the dark greens of the surrounding environment. The Larson Residence has been imaginatively reinvented to bring a touch of modernity to a historical, picturesque property.

Photography: Richard Powers

Situated in a dense urban neighborhood in Fayetteville, Arkansas, **The L-Stack House** makes extraordinary use of an otherwise difficult plot—trapezoidal in shape and cut diagonally by a dry creek bed. Designed by architect duo **Marlon** and **Meryati Blackwell** of Marlon Blackwell Architects, this exceptional home is immediately striking in its form and innovative bridging and stacking of volumes.

The block on which this house is built has been otherwise undeveloped. The result is a prominent but compact one-story home of 2525 square feet (235 square meters). The volumes comprise an L-shaped scheme of two 18-foot (5.5-meter) boxes, hinged together, with one elevated and spun 90 degrees in order to maximize the space underneath and traverse the former creek. The first floor is structured as an open linear plan, with exterior terraces that connect the indoor spaces to the creek.

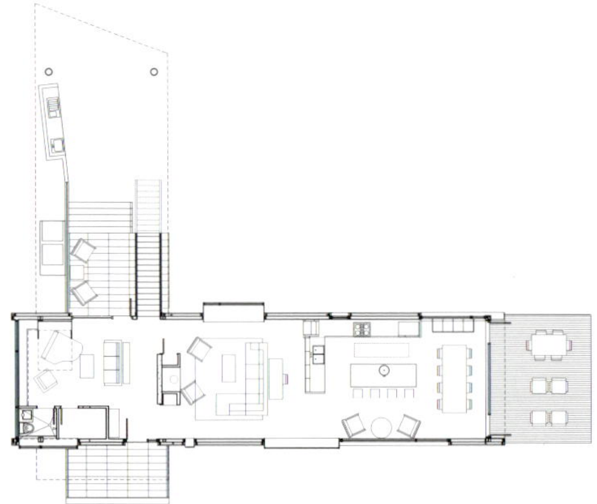

As one walks through the house, the windows and skylights are arranged so that each of them provides an intentional view of the external environment, as well as natural lighting and a sense of privacy. Private spaces are arranged on the second floor, which are more enclosed and are more discreet, while the shared spaces are experienced on the first floor. The interior is completed with wenge, walnut, and white oak millwork, painted wooden plank walls, and teak floors. One of the most interesting internal features are the large steel boxes, which are inset into the walls and hallway and protrude on the exterior, designed for sitting and sleeping.

The exterior is comprised of an innovative rain screen, expressed with rot-resistant Brazilian redwood. The end walls are constructed from either a black metal cladding or glass storefronts, resulting in a well-balanced juxtaposition in the external aesthetic of the house. The home allows the family to connect with a sense of place that reflects the changing relationship between home, the urban setting, and the environment.

Photography: *Timothy Hursley*

I THINK

The unique characteristic of **Lyon Housemuseum** is that architect and art collector **Corbett Lyon** designed it specifically to provide the public with a more intimate museum setting—one that morphs personal home with art gallery—a "housemuseum." This style allows the visitor to view the art in the context of the collector's own home, and draws its lineage from the historical art museums that are established within the former domestic setting of an artist, such as New York's Frick Collection or the Peggy Guggenheim Collection in Venice. In addition to transforming the current museological vernacular, the house also provides a novel way in which human beings can interact with art—multi-perspectivally. Corbett Lyon, one of Melbourne's multi-award-winning architects, began the design of the Housemuseum in 2007 following extensive research into existing public and private museum typologies.

The Housemuseum appears as a "white cube" at the anterior of the building and a "black box" at the posterior. Each spanning two stories, these volumes are expressed as anchors for the design. They are also creatively utilized as backdrops for the extensive collection of contemporary and postmodern art installations. The first floor is expressed as an open space that transitions cleanly through the areas of the house and opens onto landscaped courtyards that showcase further artworks. The second floor is more private, with internal windows and slit openings from which the interior of the rest of the house can be viewed.

Corbett confesses that living in the Housemuseum is challenging and interesting, and is representative of a new and speculative architectural style. The project was awarded the Australian Institute of Architects' 2010 Harold Desbrowe-Annear Award for residential architecture, and in 2013, was named one of the World's 10 Most Exciting Building of Private Art Museums by art market company Larry's List.

Photography: John Gollings and Dianna Snape

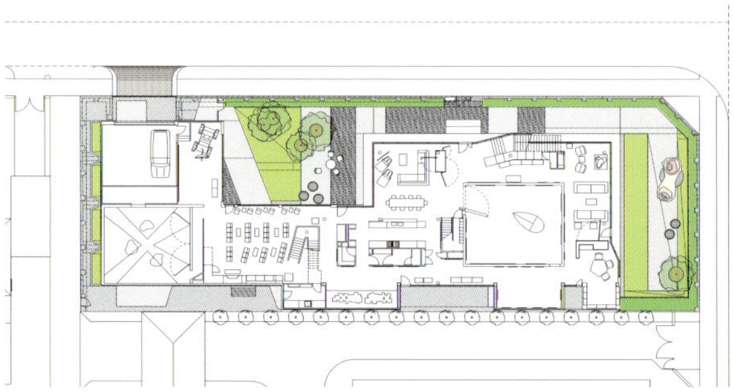

The walls and ceilings have small texts printed on to the timber paneling. These reflect some of the things that have interested us or have been important to us as a family.

Corbett Lyon

John Ruble, of Moore Ruble Yudell Architects & Planners, and his wife, architect Cecily Young, remodeled a 1950s Californian bungalow to become an open, spacious and contemporary home for themselves and their family. **Mar Vista House** is rich in Californian residential tradition, with the inclusion of several indoor-to-outdoor transitional spaces and a deep respect for the benign southern Californian climate. Being situated on an unusual, narrow but long plot allowed for an expansive private garden. This space is inspired by the courtyard gardens of Balinese architecture in Indonesia, which are organized into quadrants of different uses, and viewed from raised terraces. Otherwise the structure of this home is similar to a classic country house, but elongated and translated into a contemporary design.

The home required quite significant extensions to incorporate the architect's three-generation family. As such, the original area was almost tripled in size to a total of 4600 square feet (1400 square meters). This comprises a selection of shared spaces, including loft-like living and dining areas, a large, open kitchen, four bathrooms and bedrooms, as well as a studio. The living space and master bedroom have generous views of the garden and pool. Their open, glassy façades are oriented northeast, and protected from excessive sun by overhanging metal or fabric canopies. The entire exterior is clad with cement plaster, while the roof is composed of light metal that further minimizes solar heat gain.

The interiors thoughtfully integrate an ordered sequence of natural light, with richness of scale, and a gentle definition of space to provide the house with a comfortable flow of daily life. Despite generous extensions to the original structure, the street front of the home maintains the single-story scale of the original bungalow.

Photography: *Trevor Tondro*

Design and owned by renowned Southern Californian architect, **David Hertz**, and inspired by the multi-generational family houses in Balinese architecture on his surf travels in Indonesia, **McKinley Residence** is a sophisticated and striking example of a modern Californian home. McKinley Residence is also known as Californication House for being used as the prime location for the filming of Showtime series *Californication*.

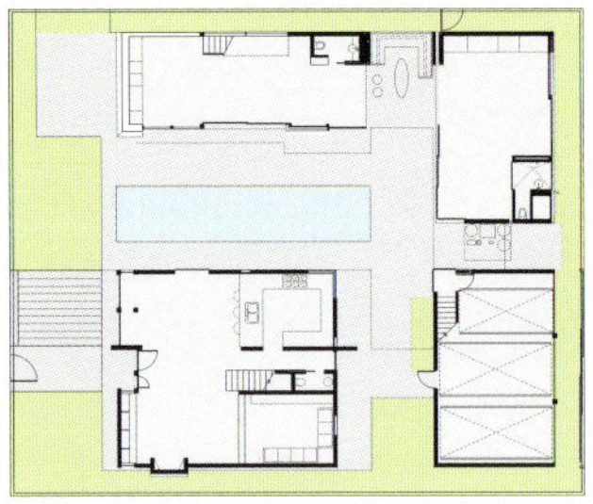

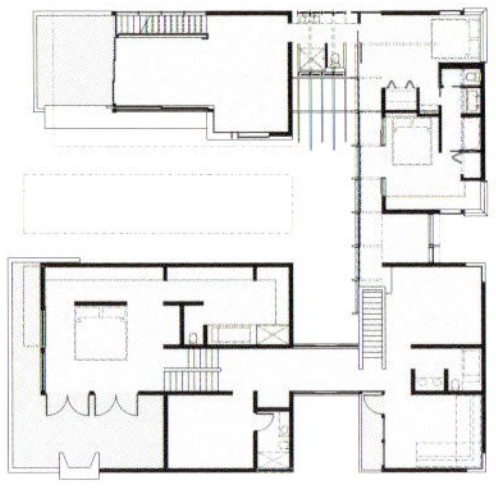

Hertz, of David Hertz Architects Inc., designed the home to take advantage of the abundant Californian light and cool ocean breeze, with plentiful windows throughout and large sliding doors that open completely—morphing the understanding of indoor and outdoor spaces. The house, which sits on what was originally two blocks, consists of four discrete buildings linked by three enclosed bridges, each facing onto a courtyard and pool.

Built in two phases, this project is a case study in green building techniques, utilizing solar energy for electricity, hot water, and radiant heating. Recycled and sustainable woods are used throughout the house, as well as Syndecrete, a concrete developed by Hertz that uses 41 percent recycled content.

The house also features passive ventilation, which eliminates the need for a forced-air system. Heat-mirror glazed windows allow for further heat management, and the house has most recently been equipped with a SkyWater atmospheric water collection system—drawing drinking water from the moisture that naturally occurs in the air.

The children's rooms are located around a home office. An outdoor shower makes it convenient to rinse off after surfing nearby Venice Beach, while the rock garden, outdoor dining table, freshwater pool and Jacuzzi all add to the house's rejuvenating atmosphere.

This house is a sophisticated and comfortable representation of the relaxed and innovative nature of modern Californian architecture.

Photography: *Shane King*

Mood Ring House is a very low-cost single family home and studio designed by architect **Marc Manack**, of SILO AR+D. Situated in an eclectic neighborhood of Fayetteville, Arkansas, walking distance from the city center, the design is a result of the limitations onsite, economic constrictions, and programmatic desires. On the plot are two prodigious Catalpa trees that Manack wished to preserve. Other programmatic requirements included orienting the house to take advantage of the northern sunlight, while also maximizing the south and west views of the forest and mountains.

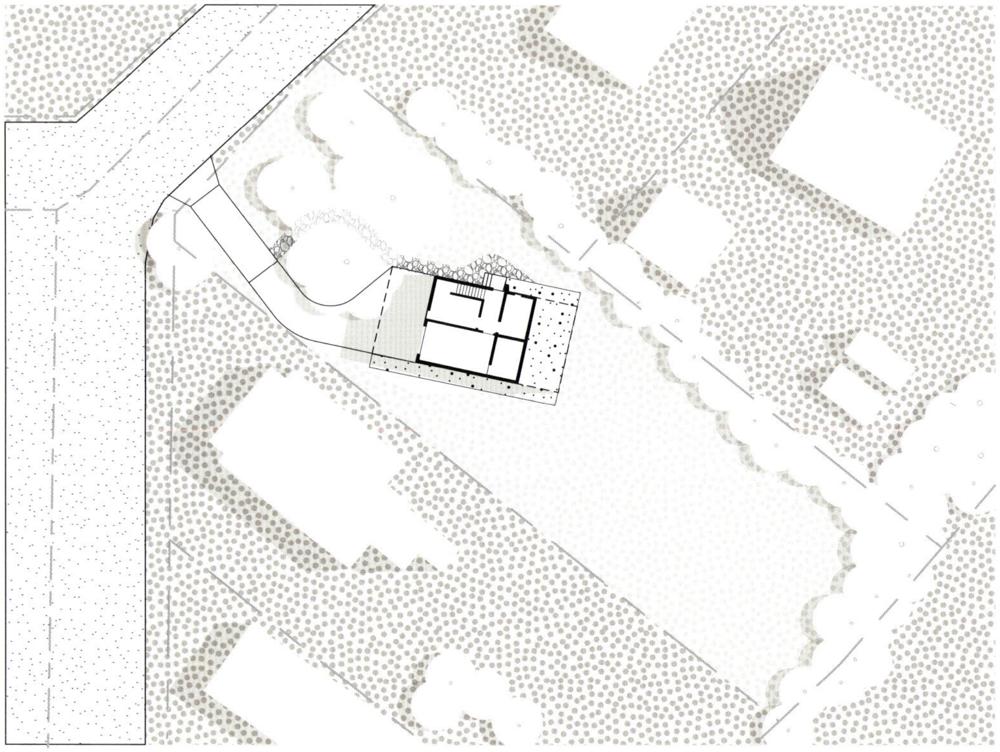

A captivating feature of this T-shaped house is the lighting of the façades as night falls. Throughout the day, the house portrays a modest character despite its expressive form, a result of the gentle textures of the materials purchased at low-cost and detailed to mask their humble character. In the evenings, the illuminated soffits create forms from the projected colorful LED light on the exterior and interior façades. These colors can be chosen by Manack and his family, creating a personal and kinesthetic connection with the space. This feature demonstrates how one piece of architecture can have a vastly differing day and night presence, using creative and unique experiential and spatial definitions.

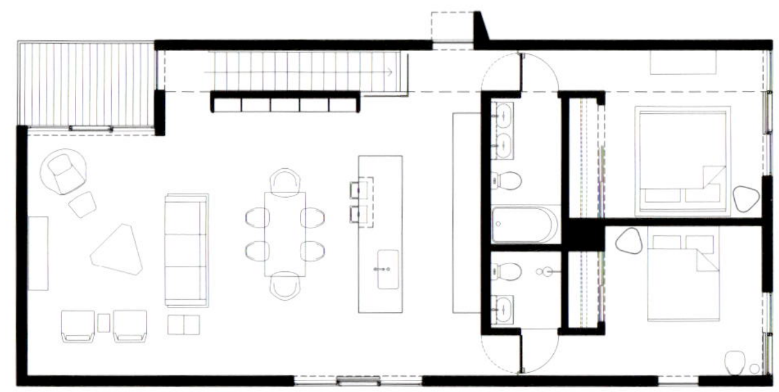

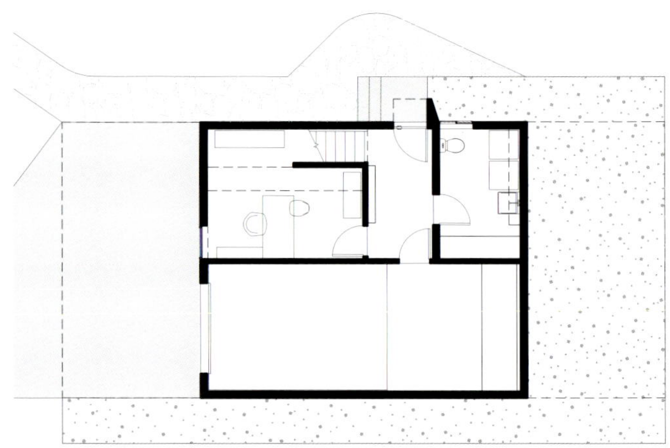

The result is a private home with a vibrant public expression. The studio areas of the home are consolidated on the first floor, with the majority of the family's living spaces concentrated on the second floor. The cantilevers and dramatic slope of the site give way to outstanding views of the natural, surrounding landscape, which can be seen from each living space. As such, the house is perfectly positioned in a private enclave among the trees.

Photography: *Timothy Hursley*

The "big sky" of the desert Southwest gives the sunlight a unique crispness and clarity, rendering amazing colors and shadows on the rocks and vegetation that shape the local topography. It is here that attracted **Michael D. Szerbaty** and his wife to the Verde Valley, Arizona, to design **Morning Sky House, Guest House and Stable**. Located in the foothills of Mingus Mountain, the steeply sloping site, densely packed with desert flora, has stunning views of the Verde Valley, Sedona, and San Francisco Peaks.

The main, 2500-square-foot (232-square-meter) house is nestled into the land at the high end of the 2.6-acre (1-hectare) site. The house is on two levels, with an open plan characterizing the upper level while the lower level is cut into the land with windows facing north. The upper floor contains the personal spaces and the main floor contains the transparent space of the living areas. A sky-lit open staircase connects upper to lower level, allowing natural light and ventilation. Sitting separately, further down the site, the horse stable and studio are similarly carved into the slope, with the 750-square-foot (70-square-meter) studio floating on piers above the landscape and stable.

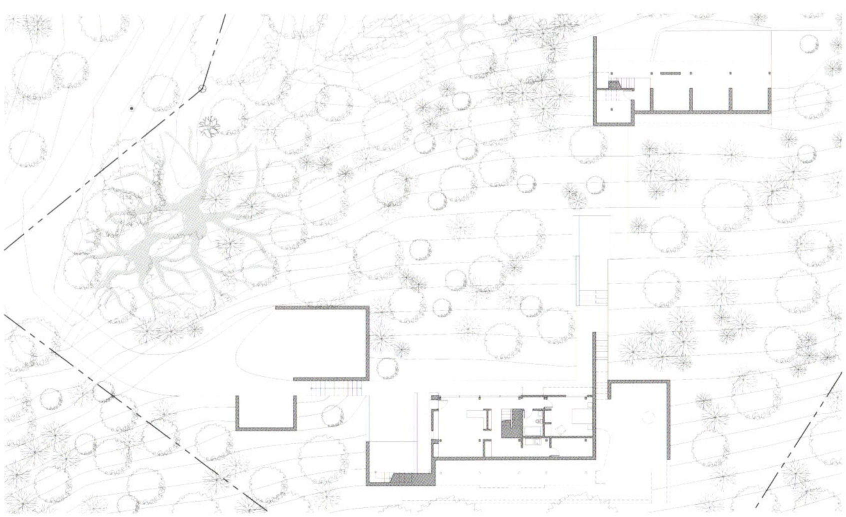

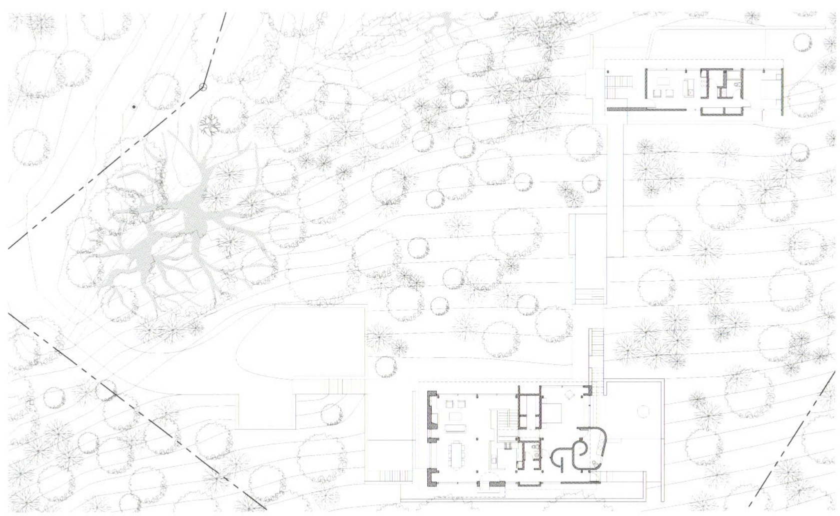

The house, incorporating earth-tone colors and natural materials such as mahogany windows, weathering steel panels, bluestone flooring and Douglas fir post and beams, is designed to "disappear" in the landscape. The large glass surfaces provide transparency, connecting inside to outside with a specific focus to views at each orientation. American Indian ruins that were constructed throughout this area, beginning in the 10th century, inspired this design. These ancient structures cut, carved and filled voids of the natural landscape, molded out of available materials such as rocks and timber. The intersecting geometries of the structures result in dynamic webs of woven grids. This project explores the meaning in such geometry overlaid on the spectacular natural landscape of the Verde Valley.

Photography: *Jon Reis with Dede Hatch*

Situated under the northern sun at the base of a dormant volcano cone, close to the Manukau harbor in Auckland, New Zealand, is where **Michael O'Sullivan** decided to design and build the **O'Sullivan Family Home**. This neighborhood is historically associated with the working class, in close proximity to the warehouses and factories surrounding the old Onehunga Wharf. Having grown up in South Auckland, O'Sullivan believes this to be one of the prettiest and most culturally diverse areas in Auckland—perfect for a home for his partner Melissa Schollum and four young children.

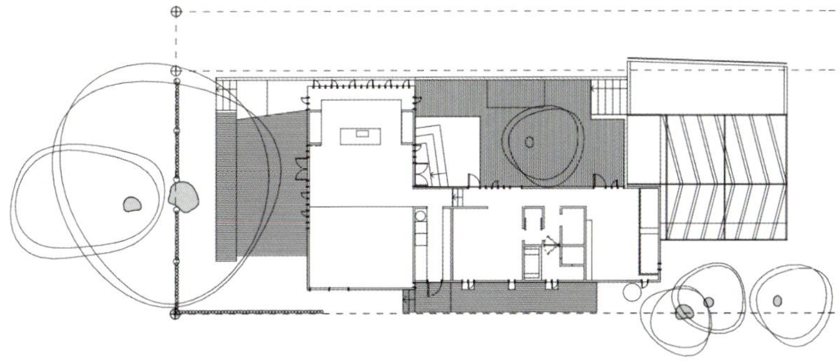

The home is a modest 1185 square feet (110 square meters) and was a first-time build for O'Sullivan. He speaks of many challenges and a few instances with an automatic nail gun throughout the build, revealing that even many years in the field do not always prepare you for your personal build. However, O'Sullivan's determination attracted the help of neighbors and friends who would spend their evenings helping with the build process. Fabricated with a very minimal budget, the home is simple in plan and elegant in form. From the street, one enters through a courtyard shaded by oak into the main living pavilion, while laundry, bathroom and bedrooms are positioned off a gallery to the back of the eastern deck. Light streams through slender windows and shutters.

O'Sullivan's countless hours spent on the build have allowed for strategic indulgences, such as exquisite green marble in the bathrooms, cedar weatherboard ceilings, and a shining brass kitchen island. Nestled in a beautiful area of Auckland, this open, welcoming and highly personal design makes for a quintessentially coastal yet urban sanctuary for O'Sullivan and his young family.

Photography: *Florence Nobel*

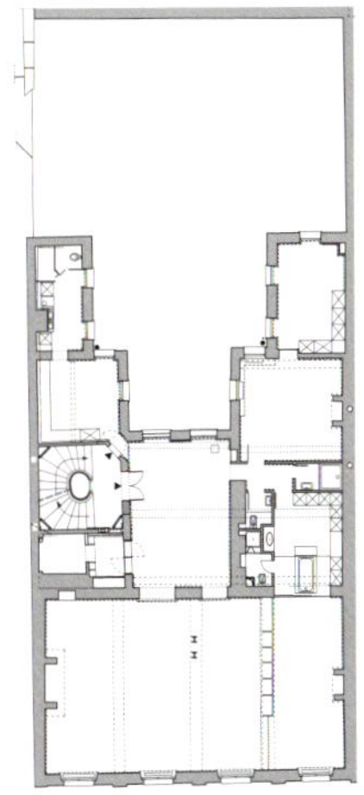

Internationally renowned Italian architects **Massimiliano** and **Doriana Fuksas**, of Studio Fuksas, selected one of the 36 brick and stone pavilions on the stunning Place des Vosges, Paris's oldest planned square, as their minimalist and sophisticated **Parisian Residence**. Historically, French ex-convict, architect and writer Fernand Pouillon once owned this home. Only minimal structural changes have been made to it since, with open plan rooms that extend throughout the house.

When settling into this large space, the Massimiliano and Doriana eliminated the existing partitions with a daring technological intrusion of steel beams to support the heavy structures of superior floors. In order to separate, symbolically, the private spaces of the reception rooms, a wall extended by shelving has been painted in Indian blue, introducing a rare tonality of color inside an environment principally composed of natural wood, metal, and bare stone. The floors, made of clear stone, welcome visitors as though it were the stage of a theater, while the objects appear to be floating in space.

Doriana has decorated the volumes with sophisticated simplicity—furniture by Jean Prouvé, some Pouillon-designed furniture that remained here for the Fuksases' use, and other emblematic creations of the technology of the 20th century. Most of the simple and functional furniture is signed by Alvar Aalto, Charlotte Perriand, Le Corbusier or Noguchi. Far from a historical reconstruction, the rooms still retain their original wood ceilings and are heated by monumental chimneys made of stone.

Photography: *Aki Furudate*

The architects of this fascinating space, **Cat Macleod** and **Michael Bellemo** (of Bellemo & Cat), wanted to create a warehouse space in which they could work and live side-by-side while still engaging with the narrow site limitations of the industrial quarter of Northcote, Melbourne, in which the house is sited. This area is full with old brick warehouses, storage spaces, and garages. Utilizing the same formal language in the design of their space, Macleod and Bellemo designed **Polygreen**, wishing to maximize the space by building three of the walls from a translucent printed skin. All but the north side, which remains glazed with a deck along its length, is covered with this skin.

The aesthetic result of these designs is two-fold. First, it allowed Macleod and Bellemo to continue their previous work from Cocoon, a personal project in Wye River, which is a lightweight monocoque structure in a coastal hamlet on the Great Ocean Road in Victoria, Australia. The imagery on the cladding of Polygreen is composed of photographs of the basket weaving that was employed in Cocoon. Second, it allows for the creation of a graphic garden that moves from the interior to the exterior spaces. Both of these elements were of crucial importance to Macleod and Bellemo throughout construction.

With a split-level plan that separates the private and workspaces, and an open plan for any shared spaces, this low-budget design makes excellent use of its allocation. The architects also implemented under-floor hydronic heating, louvered windows and a water tank. The aesthetic of the structure brings sharp and delightful greenery to the neighborhood.

Photography: *Peter Hyatt*

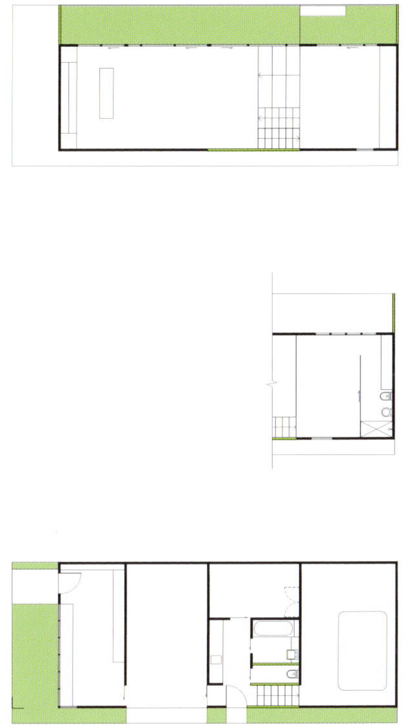

[Polygreen] enabled us to take a thread from the first cocoon we spun for ourselves in Wye River and weave it into the fabric of this next home.

Cat Macleod and Michael Bellemo

Werner Sobek designed this extraordinary four-story home on a steep section of land in Stuttgart, Germany, on the edge of a bowl-shaped valley—named **R128**. This home was designed to be completely recyclable, producing zero emissions and functioning with 100 percent self-sufficiency in regards to heating energy requirements, which are powered by solar cells. Contributing to its highly striking appearance, this modular building is completely fitted with high quality triple-glazing panels.

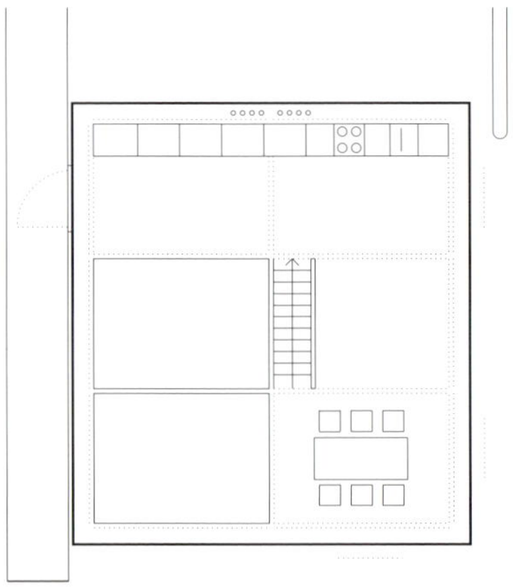

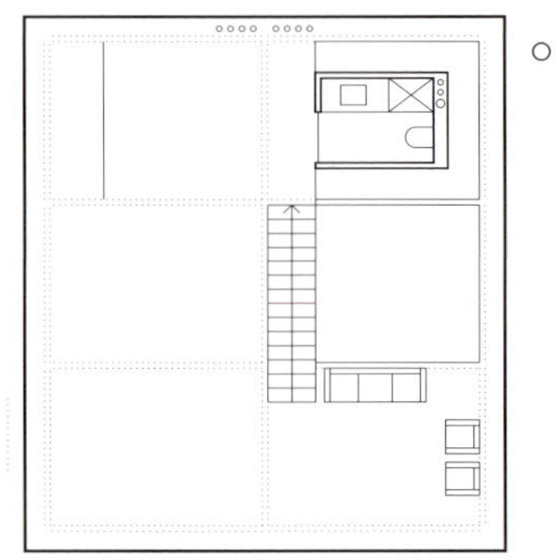

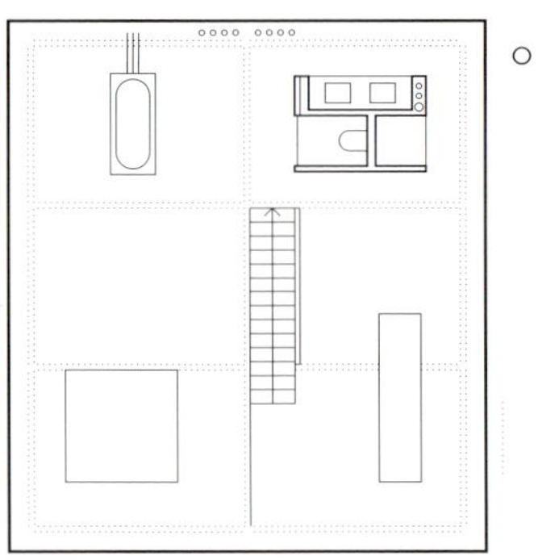

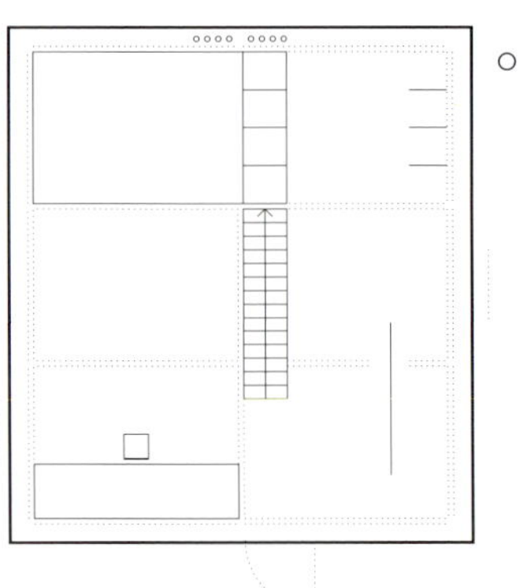

At maximum transparency, with glass panels comprising all four walls, the furniture has been kept very minimal with only a few pieces on each level. In order to access the building, one must enter and exit via a bridge that adjoins the top floor. This top level comprises the kitchen/dining space. The two levels underneath provide living and sleeping quarters, while the ground level includes the nursery and utility installations. The load-bearing structure of the building is a steel frame, reinforced by diagonals and placed on a strengthened concrete raft. No rendering or screenings were used, which eliminates the presence of any materials that are difficult to dispose of. As such, there is also a lack of pipes or cables. All supply/disposal pipe networks and communication cables are protected within metal ducts that sit against the façade.

This highly sustainable model of architecture also employs a sophisticated digital energy system—ceiling panels filled with water absorb the heat/sun energy trapped inside the building. This heat is then relocated to a heat storage unit from which the entire home is warmed through winter through a reverse of this process. With such an advanced system of sustainability and glass panels that appear to be reflecting and absorbing the bright, verdant surroundings, this home sits modestly among and within its unique and beautiful environment.

***Photography:** Zooey Braun*

Designed by world-renowned architect **Kenneth Yeang** (of T.R. Hamzah and Yeang Sdn Bhd) for himself and his family, **Roof-Roof House** is a life-size working prototype and development of his bioclimatic design principles. Yeang's goal when designing this 3500-foot-squared (325-meter-squared), two-story home in Selangor, Malaysia, was to arrange enclosed procedures—environmental filters—that support the house's minimal spatial organization and operate within the landscape. If successful, this model of infrastructure could be utilized on a larger scale, through Yeang's work as an architect.

Yeang designed the home with a north–south orientation to protect the main living areas from tropical sun, while facing the first floor living spaces east. This opens them to the poolside to capitalize on water-cooling that reduces the temperature of the southeast-to-northwest winds and modifies the internal microclimate of the home through adjustable layers. Yeang and his family adjust these in order to control privacy, ventilation, lighting, and comfort. The radial configuration of the internal spaces flow east–west and any spaces that sit in between the building and site boundary are utilized as small courtyards. Similar to an open umbrella frame, behaving like louvered sunglasses, the building has a "baffle" roof that extends beyond the flat roof of the first floor across the pool and terrace beneath. This design, acting as a filtering mechanism, is angled over the building to minimize insolation from the hot midday sun but allow for the slow warmth of the morning sun.

In a unique attempt to differentiate from other vernacular architectural approaches that were being developed at the time, Roof-Roof House is intentionally designed not as a passive house, but as a system of parts that work within the surrounding environment. As a prototype for subsequent tropical architecture, this house translates design considerations (solar heat gain, rain and wind direction and scale) into a high level functionalism.

***Photography:** K. L. Ng Photography*

The definition of home is a subjective thing with fuzzy edges and cultural particulars. This project was an exercise in testing the limits of "home" in a form and scale unfamiliar to the standard typology.

Christoph Kaiser

Architect and builder **Christoph Kaiser**, of sustainable design studio Christoph Kaiser LLC, designed, personally funded and implemented this resourceful and creative reformation of a 1955 grain silo in the Garfield Historic District of downtown Phoenix, Arizona. Named **Silo House**, there are elements of careful ingenuity sown into this compact, 366-square-foot (34-square-meter) space.

Kaiser's personal design intentions were to create a sentimental home for himself and his wife, within the compact limitations of a grain silo, wherein all design choices maintain the harmonies of the original silo structure. The design comprises two complementary sections: an interior "object" and an exterior shell (the silo frame). The interior object, a large, warm wooden and steel "machine for living," is situated within the white exterior silo structure and accommodates all basic human requirements.

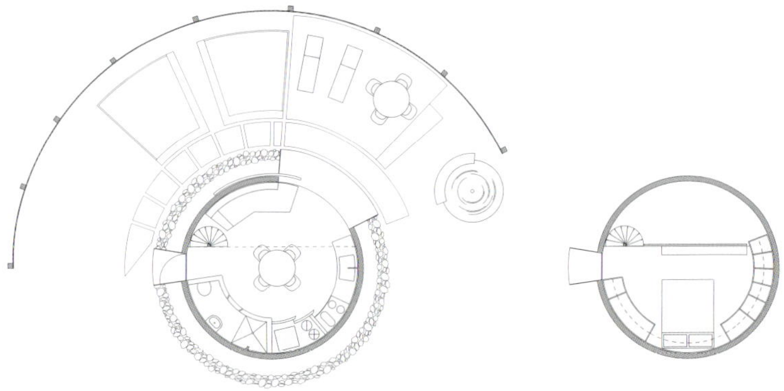

There are also considerable sustainable designs incorporated into the curved structure of the house. For example, the architecture utilizes the original cooling mechanism of the silo, whereby cool air would be sucked up through subterranean air ducts and circulated through the interior to cool the wheat or grain. This mechanism, combined with an operable skylight atop the silo, has been harnessed to deliver passive cooling for the house. Interior spaces are carefully measured, with the kitchen, bathroom and storage amenities contained within a 3-inch (7.6-centimeter) crescent that abuts the interior southern wall, maximizing floor space and spatial volume.

When asked to describe the project in three words, Kaiser chooses "compact, bold, elemental." This home, of great architectural rigor and innovative use of space and materials, is an exceptional example of the rehabilitation challenge that is of great personal significance to the architect and the community.

Photography: *Christoph Kaiser and Mark Lipczynski*

Skidmore Passivhaus, by **Jeff Stern** of In Situ Architecture, is a simple, modern home located amongst modest post-war houses in Portland, Oregon. This home seamlessly merges high-energy efficiency standards with a contemporary design. The approach to the construction was simple and direct, with a focus on efficiency and low cost. Conceived as two connected boxes, this modest, 1680-square-foot (156-square-meter) home is a certified passive house with an Earth Advantage Platinum rating, and provides the family with a true live/work condition.

There is a two-story volume for living and a single-story volume for working. The two-story space features an open plan with a loft-like master bedroom suite, while the single-story space incorporates two working studios and a shared bathroom. The space created between the volumes, while inside the thermal envelope, acts as an extension of the outdoor spacing connecting the front porch through to the rear deck. Boxy abstract forms remain clean and simple—void of cantilevers or other architectural devices. Ballooned framed walls and roofs are built on a standard module and clad in stained rough-sawn cedar. The simple and sophisticated palette comprises concrete floors, white walls, and plywood cabinets, while brightly painted doors and laminate countertops provide sharp colors.

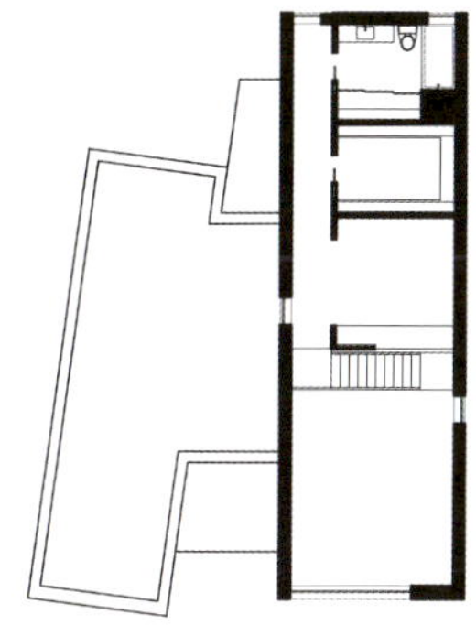

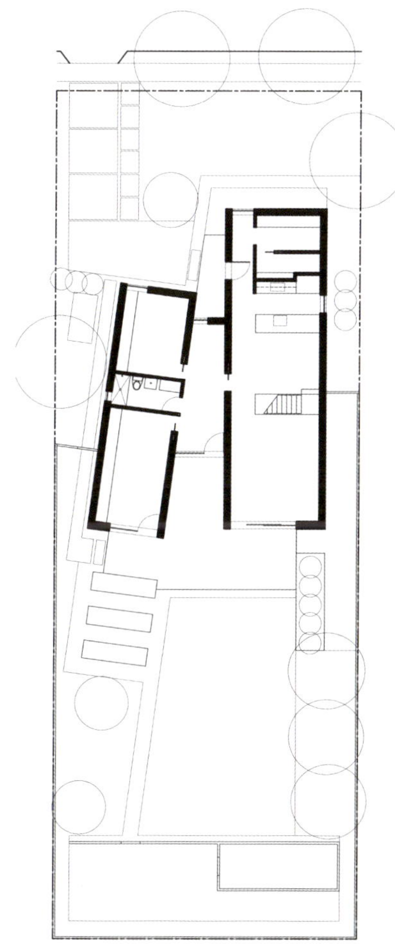

The home was constructed to be extremely airtight, resulting in the highest levels of insulation. This style of construction, coupled with triple-glazed European glass, a highly efficient heat recovery ventilator, and electric external aluminum shading that can be lowered to reflect heat gain, promises that the structure is a well-functioning passive home. A high ratio of south-facing glazing maximizes solar gains for most of the year, while an extensive green roof helps manage all storm water on site, and provides habitat for birds and insects. To complement the minimal heating load, highly efficient lighting and appliances ensure that electricity usage is maintained at lowest possible levels, while a roof-mounted photovoltaic system generates about 75 percent of the annual power supply.

Photography: *Jeremy Bittermann*

A passion for concrete as a single palette material was the inspiration for this home by **Feras Gabriel Raffoul** in Maribyrnong, Melbourne. **Skyline Drive 1** was the result of Raffoul's many years in the architecture industry, combining the ideas that he had collected and admired over the years. The result is this visually striking, three-story urban home with concrete forming the majority of the construction externally, while also being used as the main basis of the internal walls, floors, and ceilings.

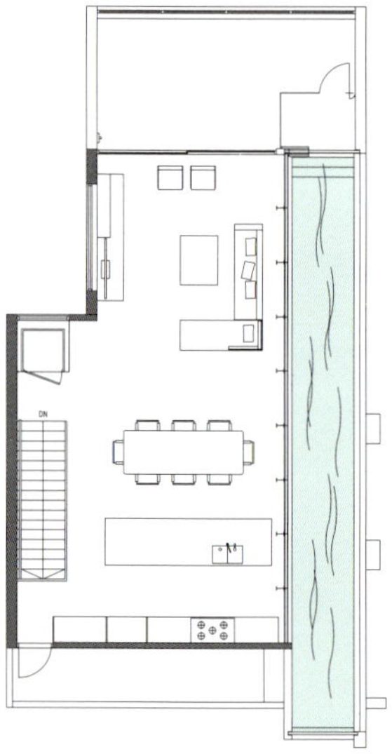

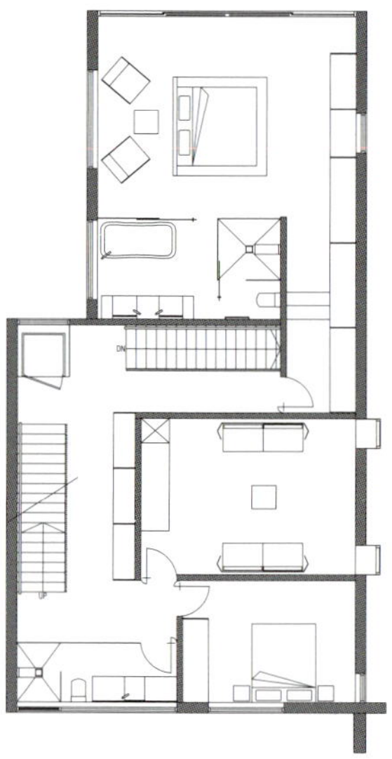

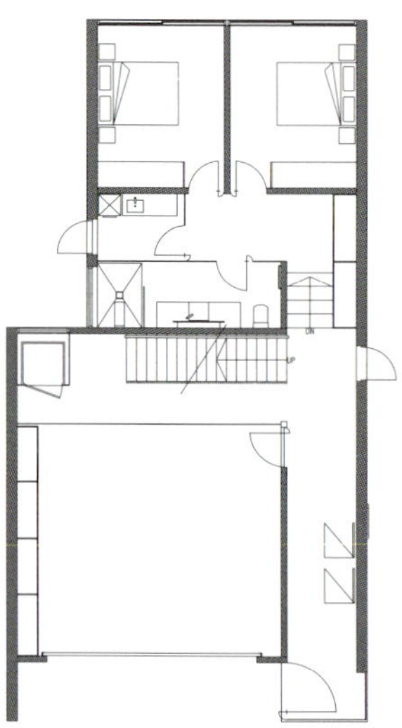

I wanted to create as bare and minimalist a design as possible.

Feras Gabriel Raffoul

Concrete, Raffoul believes, is a surprisingly warm material with efficient thermal massing qualities. The visual aesthetic of concrete, when absorbing and reflecting the shifting sunlight and external elements, creates a responsive, comfortable environment that is ever-changing. The glass roof of this home is one element that Raffoul deems to be particularly exceptional. Not only does the glass roof take advantage of the excellent views of the city of Melbourne, but it also allows the space to have a vast sense of scale as the boundaries of the interior and exterior are joined seamlessly. The ambience of the house shifts and changes as light and dark penetrate the interiors through the glass roof throughout the day. The pool on the third level, which divides the living area by an acrylic wall, is also a particular favorite of Raffoul's. This not only allows for city views to be captured whilst in the pool, but the acrylic wall also introduces the pool into the internal living space. The result is an impressive and innovative aesthetic from inside the home.

Skyline Drive 1 is an exceptional use of the elements of water and sunlight on the internal and external aesthetic of a home. Raffoul's use of polished concrete appears softened and warm with the high levels of natural light, resulting in an outstanding, contemporary design.

Photography: *Peter Bennetts*

This flexible, creative and efficient use of space exemplifies the ability to design and build within a very constricted area and still achieve maximum logicality. Occupying one of four small plots in Brixton, London, in the rear garden of a derelict house, **Slip House** by **Carl Turner** (of Carl Turner Architects; CTA) emerges as a striking sculpture in this busy British neighborhood.

Slip House appears as three flexible, "slipped" boxes that can be configured either as a single home, a studio workspace and apartment, or two separate apartments. The external walls are load-bearing which ensures that no internal supports or beams are required. Additionally, the open plan of the interior spaces ensures that the walls are movable with minimal effort. Shared living and working spaces were particularly important to CTA, and this project allowed Turner to develop not only an exceptional home, but a home that formed a prototype for a new style of urban terraced house.

Faced with no client except oneself, the project inevitably becomes a manifesto of sorts.

Carl Turner

A key functional and aesthetic feature of the house is the translucent glass façade that provides cladding for the top level as well as creating a private enclosure for the roof terrace and an amazing quality of ever-changing internal light. This milky-planked façade is what gives Slip House its interesting and creative aesthetic, while also serving a crucial function in the structure of the space. It also designed to Codes for Sustainable Homes Level 5, featuring ground source heat pumps, photovoltaic panels, a green roof, rainwater harvesting, under-floor heating, and mechanical ventilation heat recovery. Slip House is a prototype for efficient, flexible and contemporary urban housing on a dense, limited site, and is a vehicle for the in-house research of future sustainable design.

Photography: *Tim Crocker*

Domenic Alvaro, of internationally renowned studio Woods Bagot, designed **Small House** in the compact, busy alleyways of Surry Hills, Sydney, in an attempt to provide the solution to the limited footprint of an inner city block—vertical zoning. As a practice of urban consolidation, Alvaro designed this home to ascend upwards, as opposed to extending outwards, by engineering multiple and flexible uses in each individual space.

Small House is an elegant, modern and simple response to the limitations of a very compact urban block. The site measures only 20 by 23 feet (6 by 7 meters) at the base—about the same size as the garage of your typical suburban home—but stretches four stories. As a vertically zoned home, the garage and storage facilities are located at ground level, private spaces (bedrooms and bathroom) on the second floor, living areas on the third floor, shared spaces (kitchen, dining, entertainment) on the fourth, and a roof garden at the highest level, all accessed via a series of staircases. This stair space is of further assistance, allowing for air to be drawn from lower levels up through the rooftop sliding doors. Further ventilation is also offered through the large sliding windows on each level, which also maximize natural lighting and frame the Sydney skyline views. The perceived solidity of the external mass of the house provides privacy and thermal mass.

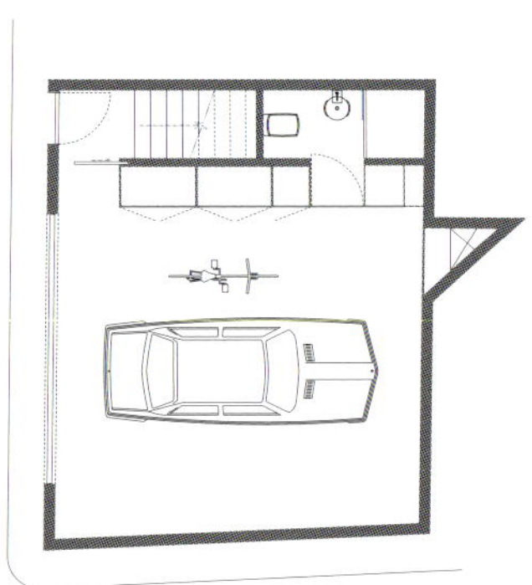

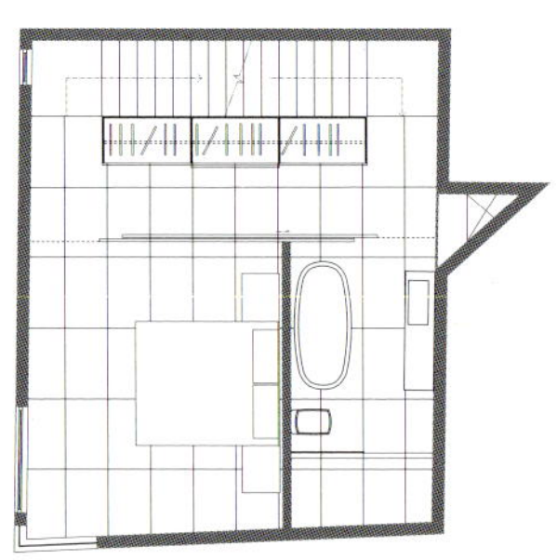

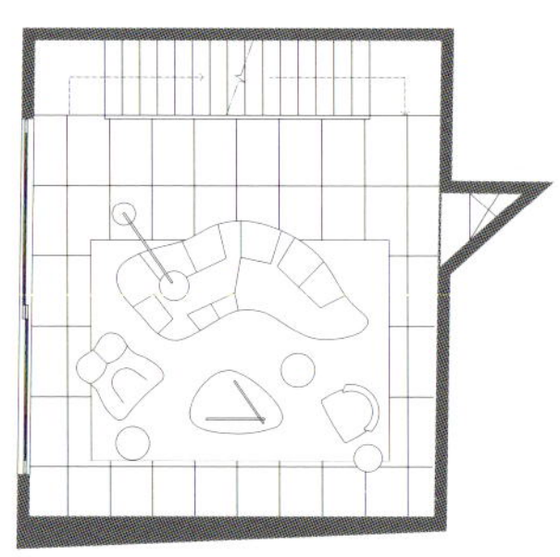

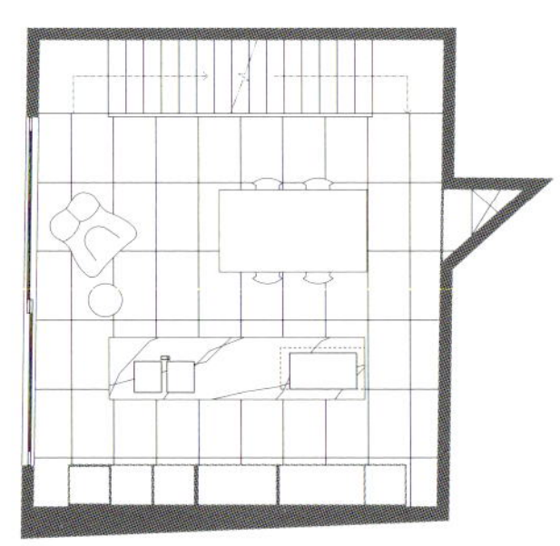

Small House is award winning for its ingenuity in an increasingly challenging urban terrain. The house has won 2011 World Architecture Festival's World House of the Year, Australian Institute of Architects' 2011 National Award for Small Project Architecture, among others. This project considers a new architectural typology while reflecting a diverse and creative contemporary lifestyle, providing an affordable and sustainable option for inner-city living.

Photography: *Trevor Mein*

From the exterior, including views from the nearby highway, this house appears as a flat shell, not dissimilar to one of the large billboards you might pass while driving there. However, the playful and creative design of the outside, together with the internal spaces is testament to the clever vision of **Philip M Dingemanse** when designing the eminently personal **Southern Outlet House**. This home was designed with particular attention to the opportunities and consequences that arise when the owner is also the architect and builder.

Southern Outlet House is intended to represent the contribution that a private home can make to the public sphere in which it is situated. Dingemanse adopts an early-20th-century technique in naval camouflage in order to allow the front façade to "dazzle." This not only manipulates the public-facing side, but also helps to adjust the home's scale, while the reflection of lights from the façade apply an extra dimension to an otherwise flat front, and define the roof edge of the building. As a stark contrast to this external aesthetic, the interior timbers allow a textual warmth and open volume to the family's space.

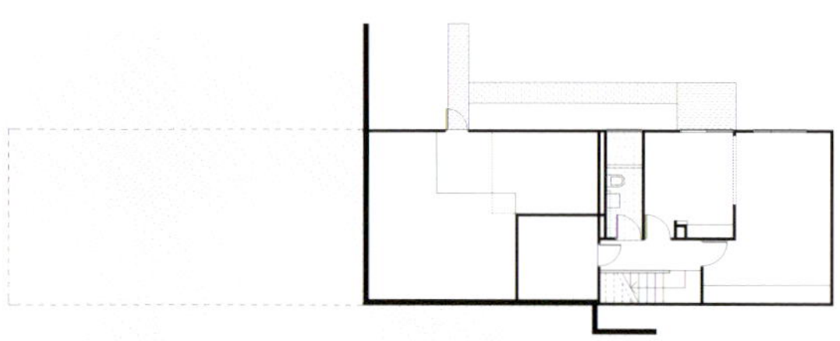

Though reasonably small in floor area, all opportunities of the building section are maximized. As it is a steep site, the building is required to stretch across the sloping land with a continuous, straight roofline that eventually carries two stories underneath. Higher in the volume is a studio space that allows views across the living area. There are also opportunities for intimacy in this open space—a workbench shelters a sunken lounge below, forming a ceiling that allows privacy within the larger volume. With the addition of extensive gardens, light-filled spaces, sustainable architecture, and ample family space, Southern Outlet House represents the possibilities when all decisions and responsibilities are attributed to designing one's house oneself.

Photography: *Jonathan Wherrett*

Steinhaus (Stone House) is the outstanding and monumental design of late Austrian architect **Günther Domenig**. Begun in 1986 and finally completed in 2008, in the mountains of Carinthia, Austria, this design is crucial in the development of modern architecture. Steinhaus represents the transformation of regional landscape elements that led to an architectural sculpture with a clear intensity of form.

The sharp, angular linearity and darkened, reflective panels are self-confessed representations of the extension of Domenig's personality and art through architecture—a manifesto of his skill and experimentation with form. This home is sited on a narrow edge of a lake. The house was continually added to, following the evolution of a series of sketches and technical drawings. Now one of the most famous homes in Carinthian contemporary architecture, it acts as a structural biography for Domenig.

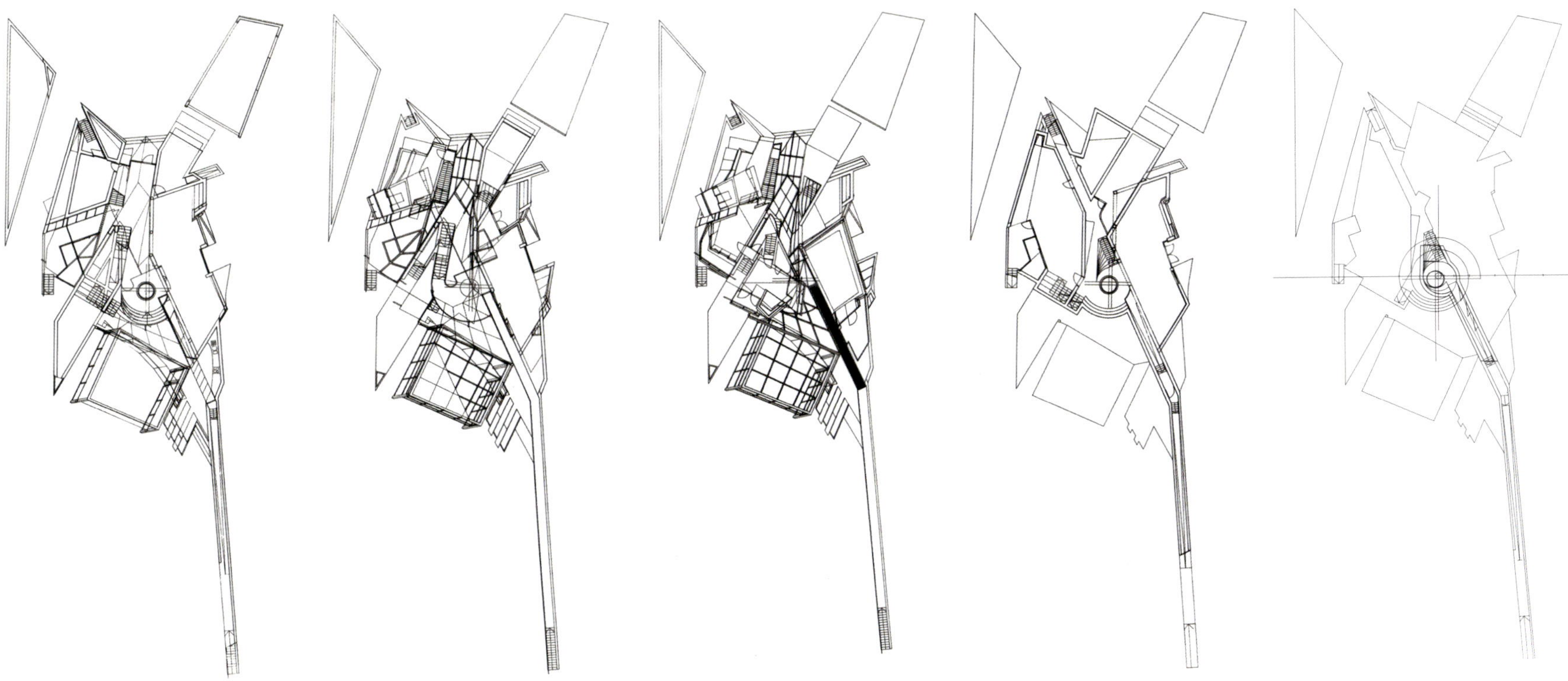

Steinhaus was designed with the intention of providing a research workshop for architects to connect with professionals from other disciplines, such as art, culture, music, and literature. A program of guided tours, symposia, workshops and cultural events now utilize the inspiring density of the space.

Photography: *Helga Rader, Gerhard Maurer*

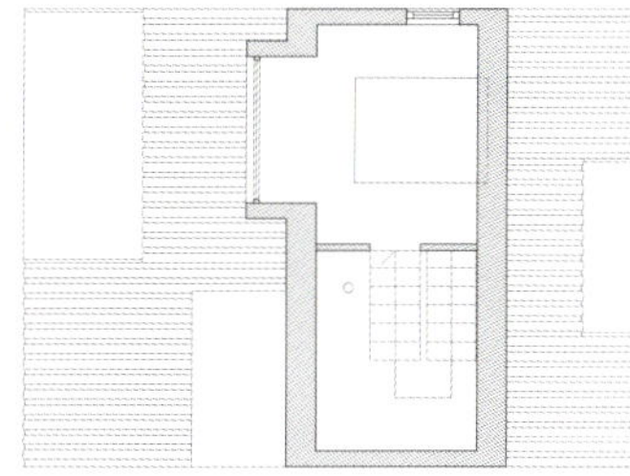

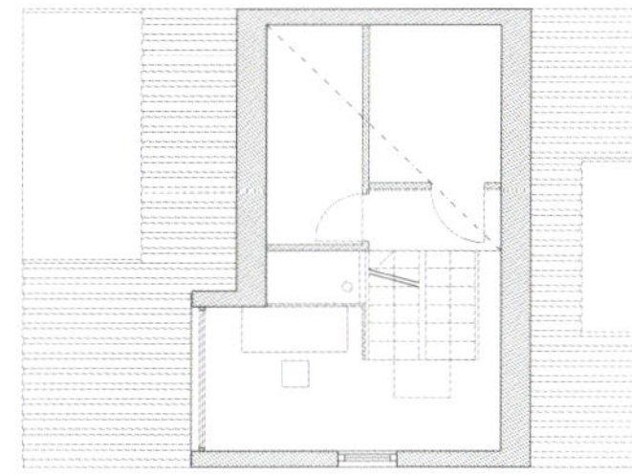

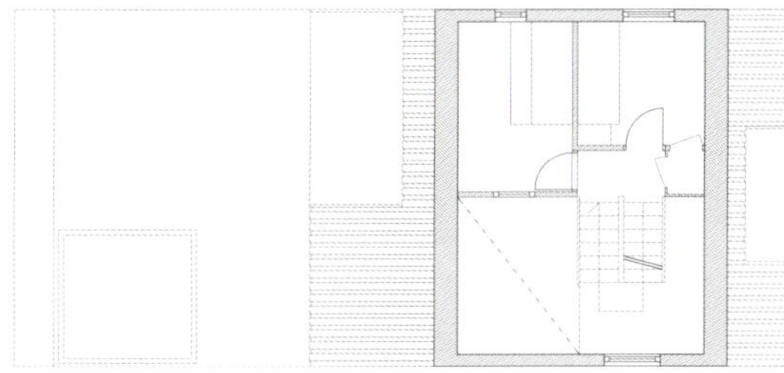

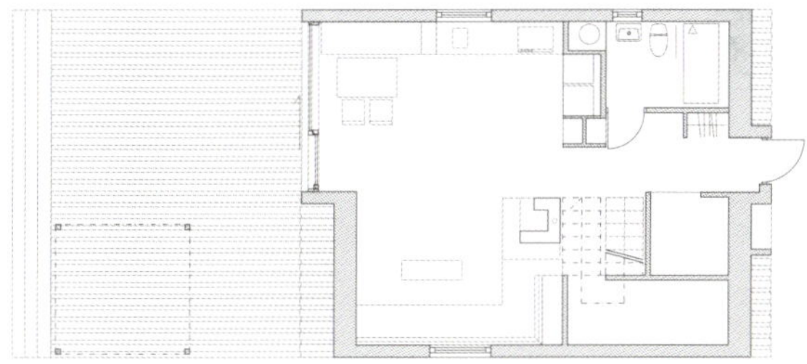

Simple yet deceptively challenging objectives underline the creation of this very personal project, **Summer House in Dalarna**—a quiet place to read, a bedroom under the stars, and the facilities to cook both indoors and outdoors. **Leo Qvarsebo** designed this picturesque, unassuming house for himself and his young family in the historical province of Dalarna in Sweden.

This modest retreat manifests each of its three personal objectives—reading, sleeping and cooking—under bay windows that permeate a sharp angled roof, which slopes down to become a comfortable terrace in front of the house. With a total surface of approximately 915 square feet (85 square meters), the house comprises eight rooms in total, including two huts and three terraces. Each of the five levels are linked with a zigzag stairway.

Made completely from wood, and nestled into the forest line at the edge of a former cow pasture plot, the house appears as somewhat of a tree house for adults and children alike. Qvarsebo wanted to ensure that this project not only allowed for the capitalization of its excellent views, but also for a close relationship between its inhabitants and the environment. As you climb to the top of the outside slope of the house roof, you can see the cow pastures and sea to the south and a dense forest to the north.

The house is rich with personal character. The A-shaped structural frame of the house is built from wooden beams while the exterior roof and walls are made from Swedish pine. Interiorly, the ceiling, floor, walls and furniture are all clad with plywood from an old jigsaw puzzle factory, while the windows and doors are all secondhand furnishings.

Photography: *Åke E:son Lindman*

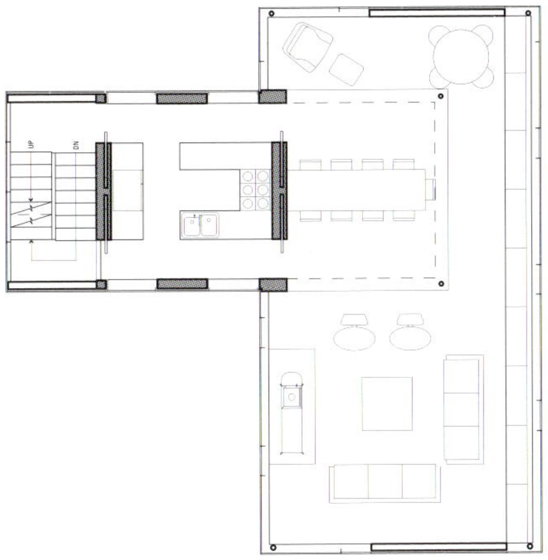

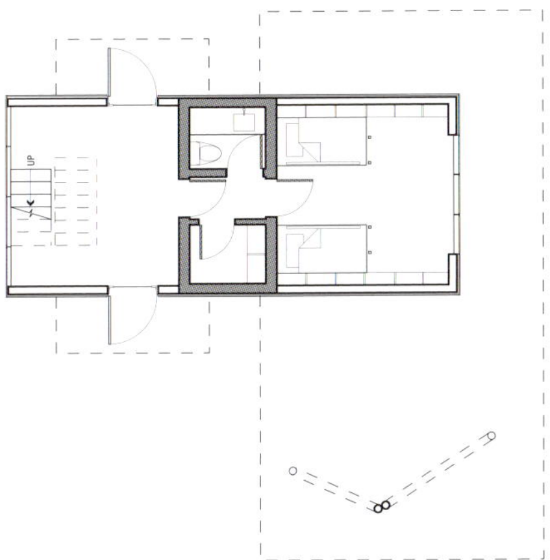

New York-based architect **Thomas Gluck**, with GLUCK+, designed this impressive structure as a vacation home for his family—as a stairway to the canopy of trees that fill this site in upstate New York. With stretching views of the Catskill mountain range, the 2545-square-foot (236-square-meter) **Tower House** was designed with a simple objective—to build an energy-efficient, sustainable retreat that reduces its cost and maintenance throughout the year. The cantilevered design becomes both a lookout and a family retreat while maintaining the smallest footprint possible.

Each of the first three levels comprises only one small, personal suite, with a modest sleeping space and bathroom. On the top level—elevated 30 feet (9 meters) above the ground—is the living space that stretches across the extension of the whole floor. An external deck on the roof of the house pushes the living spaces horizontally further into the canopy, allowing magnificent views of the mountains and lake.

A dual-sustainability strategy was implemented in order to improve temperature control. First, by organizing the wet zones of the house into an insulated central core, much of the house can be "turned off" when not in use, saving on energy use and operating costs. Second, the south-facing glass of the stairwell creates a solar chimney to take advantage of the stack effect to exhaust hot air out the top and draw fresh air through the house for natural ventilation. A key element of the design, the glass-enclosed staircase, with its glazed, back-painted skin, also reflects back each layer of the rising canopy out to the observer. At night, with a few lights on inside, the house twinkles inside its surrounding treescape.

Photography: *Paul Warchol and GLUCK+*

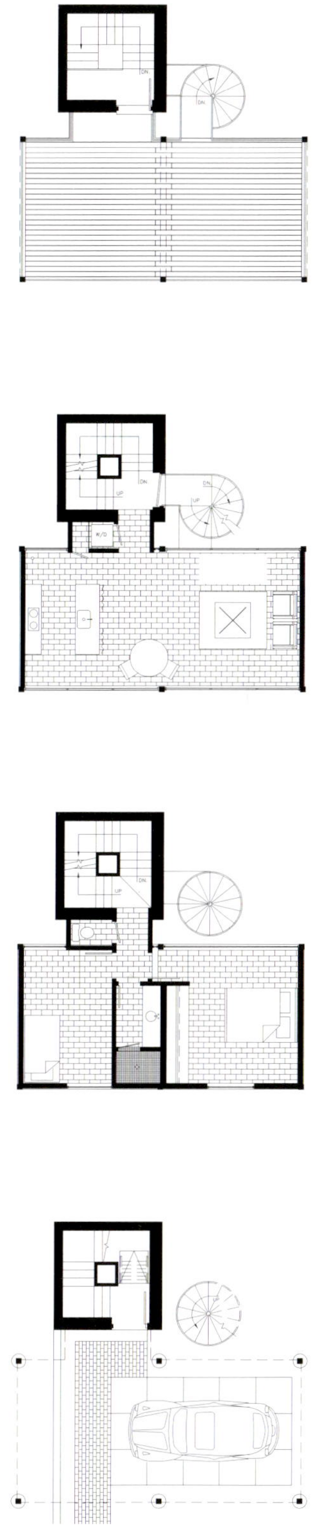

This home is exemplary of the creativity that is required to maintain a high standard of sustainability while maximizing the space of a very small site. **Tower House (Chicago)**, designed for himself by architect **Rick Phillips**, combines simple modernity with the modest footprint of a small-house scheme.

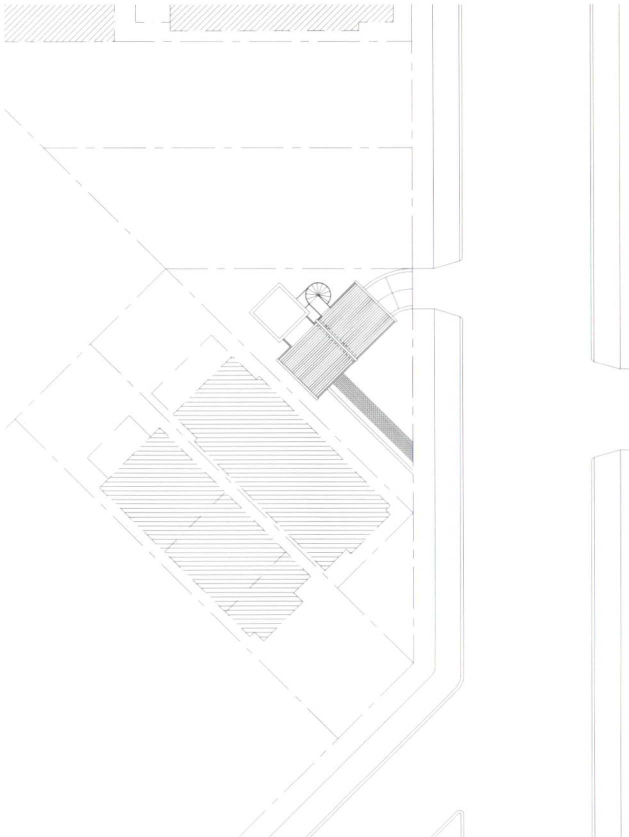

Constructed on an irregular lot, this 1200-square-foot (111-square-meter) house is situated on the southern edge of Chicago's Old Town neighborhood. The home comprises two key components: an exposed steel structure that spans the four-story volume on a 10-foot (3-meter) square and a 40-foot-high (12-meter-high) concrete masonry stair tower that links the floors. Interestingly, the house is also positioned at a 45-degree angle to the street. As a result, the upper floors have the privilege of an expansive view of the Chicago skyline, which inspired Phillips to intentionally invert the layout of the spaces. All principal outdoor areas are situated on the roof terrace of the fourth level; the living, dining and kitchen areas sit on the third level; bedrooms are located on the second level; and parking and access to the masonry tower on the first level. As an addition to the interesting visual aesthetic of the structure, the first and fourth floors are completely open to the outside, while the second and third floors are enclosed. Throughout the construction, the sustainability of the structure was important to Phillips. The structure includes translucent awnings to minimize solar heat gain, in-floor heating under slate floors, and polished concrete masonry units.

This simplicity and precision of the form and function that this home represents is demonstrated through the creative manipulation that Phillips employs in such a small space. The result is an innovative small-home design with exceptional views and naturally comfortable interior expression.

Photography: William Kildow

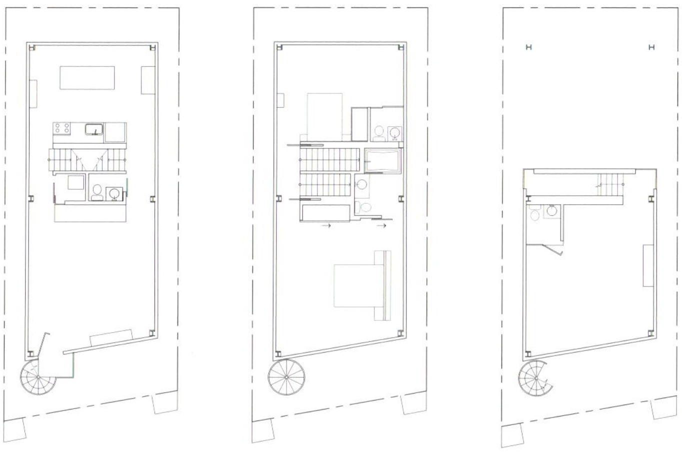

The form and shapes that have been utilized in the design of this project inspire its definitive character and unique approach to urban infill. Usually, an undeveloped urban site such as this might be oriented in terms of front and back yards, within its surroundings. However, when **Lorcan O'Herlihy**, of Lorcan O'Herlihy Architects (LOHA), chose to include window slits on all walls of the exterior façade of **Vertical House**, the result was a building that interacts with its existing neighborhood on all sides.

Vertical House occupies 2400 square feet (222 square meters) and is sited on a block in Venice, California, with very limiting characteristics. The height of the building is dictated by the lack of horizontal allocation at ground level. While the window slits appear random, they have been meticulously considered and proportioned to allow for particular views from the interior. The structure into which they have been inserted is one steel frame with Profilit™ channel glass and reinforced fiberboard panels. The rhythm of the openings is a powerful statement on the form, materiality and surface control of this house, and conveys the significant contribution of the external skin to the internal functioning of a space.

A vertical core stabilizes the internal circulations, maintaining a steady center from which the walls can pull, opening the large interior spaces and aligning them to a shared point. The staircase sits within this core, which allows access to all levels and the roof. The roof level comprises a reading area and an external deck that faces the Pacific Ocean.

***Photography:** Jurgen Nogai, Lorcan O'Herlihy Architects, and Michael Weschler*

Canadian-born architect **Todd Saunders** has been living in Bergen for 18 years, surrounded by fjords and mountain ranges on the southwestern coast of Norway. The influence of the Scandinavian architecture glimmers through the design and decorations of this house—the personally designed home of Saunders—named **Villa S**.

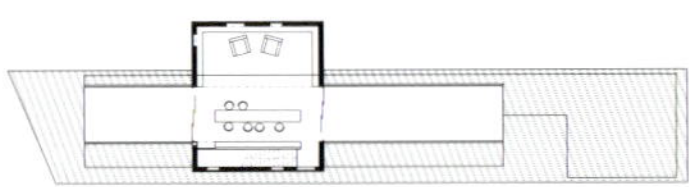

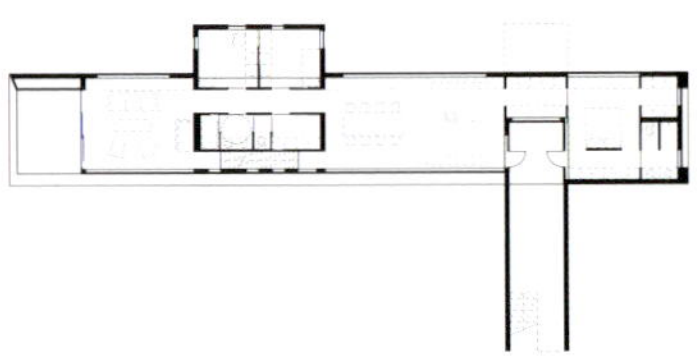

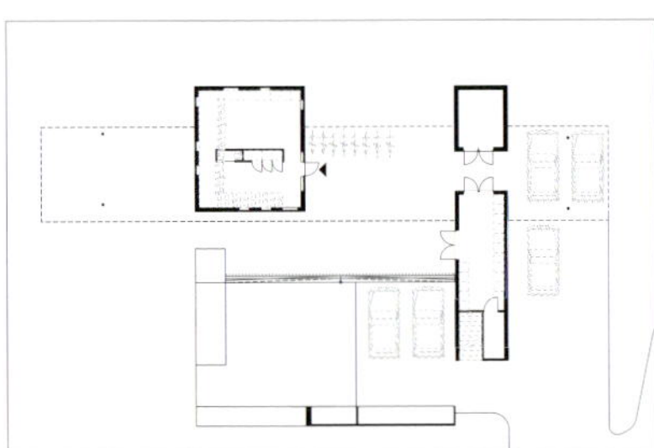

I approached it as a home for my family, to make our life really good.

Todd Saunders

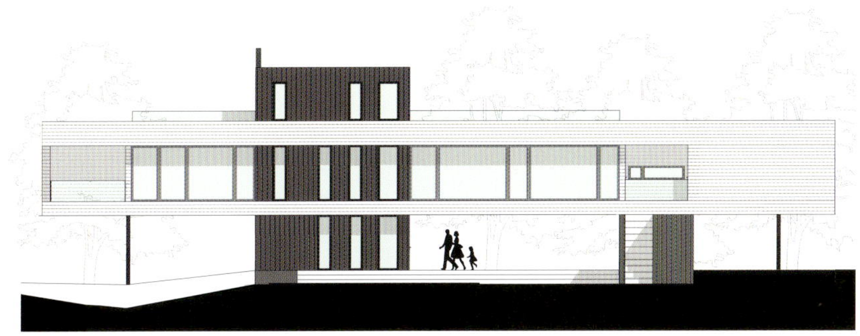

Situated among a community of modern villas called Tveiterås Garden City, which lies south of the Bergen city center, this 3230-square-foot (300-square-meter) home is described by Saunders as "three sticks, stacked on top of each other." The form of the house comprises three wood-clad volumes—two horizontally and one vertically stacked. The vertical volume includes the custom-built staircase, while the horizontal expansion encompasses the kitchen at its core with a master suite to the west, two bedrooms toward the center, and a 115-foot (35-meter) living area stretching to the east. This east–west orientation pays homage and respect to the traditional style of housing in this neighborhood.

One can appreciate that this may be the home of an architect when you begin to notice the intricate details of functionality—spatial trickeries, secret alignments, large terraces, and other details. A sophisticated aesthetic is created in the long, elegant interior spaces, with a rectilinear synchronicity that is matched between the white paneled roofs, Dinesen wooden floors, and a straight 30-foot (9-meter) kitchen counter. The interiors and furniture was selected from North American and Scandinavian design studios in collaboration with Swedish artist Hannes Wingate. A library sits on the top floor, which is a modest extravagance within a house that Saunders describes as "the closest I've come to bringing architecture and home together." It is a highly styled, simple and contemporary home with recognizable personal touches in every element of the design.

Photography: *Bent René Synnevåg*

Inspired by the placement, movement and observation of natural elements such as clay, sand, wind, and rain, **Welham Studios** searches for a triangulation of architecture, the environment, and our place between these two dynamics. Designed by renowned architect **Mark Merer** for himself and his wife, artist Lucy Glenginning, Welham Studios was developed as an environmentally sensitive project that sits within its landscape, instead of above or beneath it.

The inspiration for this studio developed from a previous housing project conducted in collaboration with the Swinomish Indian Tribal community on Fidalgo Island in the United States. This project, entitled Landhouse, saw Merer working with collaborating architects to develop a 'longhouse', a structure traditional to the Swinomish people, which actively interacts with the landscape. Encouraged by these constructions, Merer began to design a space that would interact this way with the English landscape. Welham Studios is assembled from insulated panels from the same Seattle-based factory that provided the materials for Landhouse. The design also utilizes Thermoform cladding, an EPDM-membrane roof with built-in root barrier, and a 3-inch (76-millimeter) substrate with a wildflower turf.

Welham Studios is a progressive design that incorporates deep-rooted housing traditions in order to negotiate the critical relationship between human beings and their environments. Nestled neatly and comfortably into the earth, the striking linearity of the design and color creates a studio that reflects Merer's creativity and open-mindedness.

Photography: *Louis Porter*

Located in the north Brisbane suburb of Wooloowin in Queensland, Australia, **Wooloowin House** is a unique and bold extension to a traditional 1900s residential cottage. Architect **Terry McQuillan**, of bureau^proberts, intended to design a home that was sensitive to the heritage of the original building, while creating a space that his family could call their own. The front façade, historical in nature, is the result of McQuillan's sensitive refurbishment, which bears almost no resemblance to the home's dramatic extension. He and his wife were determined to create a new, strong connection with the outdoors and to maximize light, cross benches and the available space beneath the house.

McQuillan's response is a weatherboard-clad, two-story extension separated from the original cottage by a louvered breezeway on the western side. Incorporated in the addition is a new kitchen, a master bedroom, an outdoor living space at the upper level, and a gymnasium and carport at the lower level. As an integral part of the design, the new addition boasts a strong connection to the outside, drawing in a significant amount of natural light and ventilation, the latter having a dramatic cooling effect on the home's internal temperature.

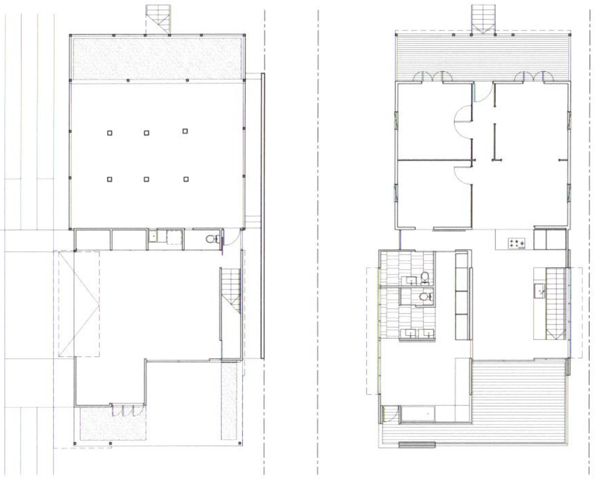

*The simplicity of the design …
and the transition space
between the original house
and the extension highlights
the character of the old cottage.*

Terry McQuillan

The extension has been crafted in such a way that it achieves a high level of privacy, despite the largely open-space planning. The sliding wall panels were designed to create partitions that closed off sections of the house not being used, ensuring privacy for the rooms while opening them up to the outdoors. "The concept was to transform the simple cottage into a stylish modern home," he explains, "however, it was important that the character of the cottage was retained and that the extension utilized materials that were sympathetic to the original."

***Photography:** Alicia Taylor*

Upon deciding to relocate from a large rural location to the city, **Buzz Yudell** and **Tina Beebe** designed this highly ecological space in which they could drive their own goals for a sustainable lifestyle while using the home as an experimental opportunity that might inform their future architectural projects. **Yudell/Beebe House** evolves as a "yin-yang" pattern with the interior and exterior environments growing to complement and intersect with one another. This pattern transforms an otherwise tight plot by inviting diagonals and line movements to interrupt the linear rigidity of the space.

One of the key features of this home is the translucent canopy that provides shading and shape to the outdoor spaces, which comprise an outdoor "tea room" and outdoor dining area. At twilight, the canopy is alight from interior illumination, as well as pinpoint lighting, that re-designs the reflections within the space. The central, two-story structure is essential to the environmental validity of the home, while also functioning as a conduit that links all internal spaces together. Each of the spaces with exposure to the two-story space has the benefit of soft daylight exposure and indirect twilight.

Acting both as designers and clients enabled us to treat the project as a case study in which creating a place of harmony aligned with ambitious environmental goals.

Buzz Yudell and Tina Beebe

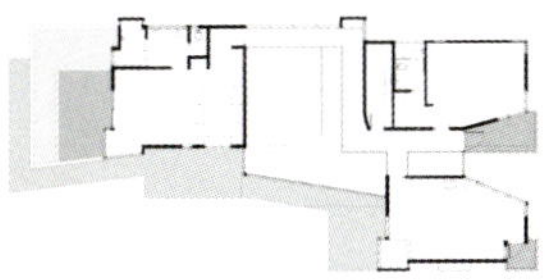

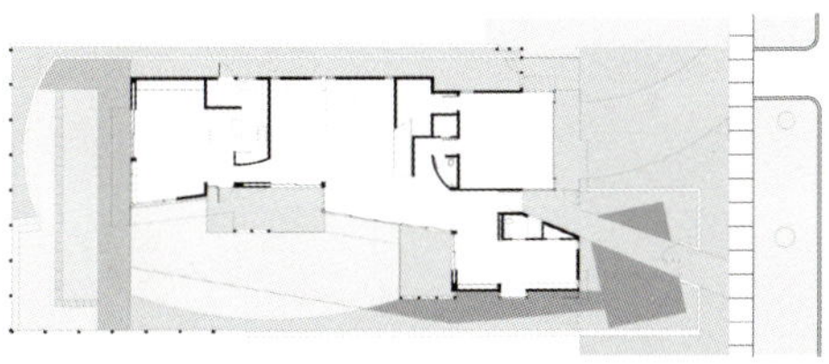

The designers also found that with an increased awareness of sustainable design they were able to further develop transitional spaces that maximized the subtle experiences of the natural elements. The sustainable approach to the design of this home was multilayered, with the inclusion of: passive design, renewable energy installations, drought-resistant landscape design, low-environmental-impact material sourcing, and system monitoring for any future environmental adjustments or technologies that could be implemented. As a continually adapting environment, and a comforting space in which the designers can envisage their own professional development, it is clear that this home serves an important dual-function—inspiration and nurturing.

Photography: *Colins Lozada and David Marlow*

Index of Architects

Domenic Alvaro
SMALL HOUSE (page 162)
Woods Bagot
woodsbagot.com

Marlon and Meryati Blackwell
THE L-STACK HOUSE (page 92)
Marlon Blackwell Architects
marlonblackwell.com

Paolo Carlesso
CASA CM (page 40)
Paolo Carlesso Studio
ec2.it/paolocarlesso

Philip M Dingemanse
SOUTHERN OUTLET HOUSE (page 167)
Philip M Dingemanse Architecture + Design
pmd.net.au

Günther Domenig
STEINHAUS (page 172)
Architektur Haus Kärnten
architektur-kaernten.at

Timothy Eddy
ASH+ASH (page 30)
Hennebery Eddy Architects
henneberyeddy.com

Ben Edwards
DOLL'S HOUSE (page 50)
Edwards Moore
edwardsmoore.com

Andreas Fuhrimann and Gabrielle Hächler
APARTMENT AT THE FOOT OF THE ÜETLIBERG MOUNTAIN (page 13)
Andreas Fuhrimann Gabrielle Hächler Architekten
afgh.ch

Massimiliano and Doriana Fuksas
PARISIAN RESIDENCE (page 127)
Studio Fuksas
fuksas.it

Antón García-Abril
HEMEROSCOPIUM HOUSE (page 73)
Ensamble Studios
ensamble.info

Thomas Gluck
TOWER HOUSE (page 183)
GLUCK+
gluckplus.com

David Hertz
McKINLEY RESIDENCE (page 107)
David Hertz FAIA Architects
davidhertzfaia.com

Mark and Angela Jamison
BIRD HOUSE (page 36)
Jamison Architects
jamisonarchitects.com.au

Christoph Kaiser
SILO HOUSE (page 145)
Christoph Kaiser LLC
christophkaiser.com

Ismet Khambatta and Bimal Patel
ISMET–BIMAL RESIDENCE (page 77)
HCP Design Planning & Management
hcp.co.in

Douglas Larson
LARSON RESIDENCE (page 89)
Larson and Paul Architects LLP
larsonandpaul.com

Corbett Lyon
LYON HOUSEMUSEUM (page 99)
Lyons Architecture
lyonsarch.com.au
lyonhousemuseum.com.au

Cat Macleod and Michael Bellemo
POLYGREEN (page 131)
Bellemo & Cat
bellemocat.com

Marc Manack
MOOD RING HOUSE (page 110)
SILO AR+D
siloard.com

Robert Maschke
C-HOUSE (page 47)
Robert Maschke Architects
robertmaschke.com

Terry McQuillan
WOOLOOWIN HOUSE (page 209)
bureau^proberts
bureauproberts.com.au

Mark Merer
WELHAM STUDIOS (page 202)
markmerer.co.uk

Jetty and Maarten Min
DUNE HOUSE (page 54)
Min2
min2.nl

Lorcan O'Herlihy
VERTICAL HOUSE (page 191)
Lorcan O'Herlihy Architects (LOHA)
loharchitects.com

Michael O'Sullivan
O'SULLIVAN FAMILY HOME (page 121)
Bull/O'Sullivan Architecture Ltd
bosarchitecture.co.nz

Shane Pavonetti
GARDEN STREET RESIDENCE (page 61)
Pavonetti Architecture
pavonettiarchitecture.com

Armin Pedevilla and Caroline Willeit
CHALET LA PEDEVILLA (page 80)
Pedevilla Architects
lapedevilla.it

Rick Phillips
TOWER HOUSE (CHICAGO) (page 187)
Frederick Phillips & Associates
frederickphillips.com

Leo Qvarsebo
SUMMER HOUSE IN DALARNA (page 177)
Leo Qvarsebo Arkitekt MSA
leoqvarsebo.se

Feras Gabriel Raffoul
SKYLINE DRIVE 1 (page 152)
fgrarchitects.com.au

Manit and Sonali Rastogi
ARCHITECTS' HOUSE + STUDIO (page 18)
Morphogenesis
morphogenesis.org

Thomas Roszak
GLASS HOUSE (page 65)
roszak.com

John Ruble
MAR VISTA HOUSE (page 103)
Moore Ruble Yudell Architects & Planners
moorerubleyudell.com

David Saunders
ARGYLE (page 25)
s2 design
s2design.com.au

Todd Saunders
VILLA S (page 194)
Saunders Architecture
saunders.no

Werner Sobek
R128 (page 134)
Werner Sobek
wernersobek.com

Jeff Stern
SKIDMORE PASSIVHAUS (page 149)
In Situ Architecture
insituarchitecture.net

Michael D. Szerbaty
MORNING SKY HOUSE, GUEST HOUSE AND STABLE (page 114)
Michael D. Szerbaty Architect, MDSzerbaty Associates Architecture
mdsync.com

Carl Turner
SLIP HOUSE (page 158)
Carl Turner Architects
ct-architects.co.uk

Federica Vasetti
GREENBANK ROAD (page 69)
Dittrich Hudson Vasetti Architects
dhva.co.uk

Kenneth Yeang
ROOF-ROOF HOUSE (page 140)
T.R. Hamzah and Yeang Sdn Bhd
hamzahyeang.com

Buzz Yudell and Tina Beebe
YUDELL/BEEBE HOUSE (page 216)
Moore Ruble Yudell Architects & Planners
moorerubleyudell.com